Scrapbooking Baby's Cherished Moments

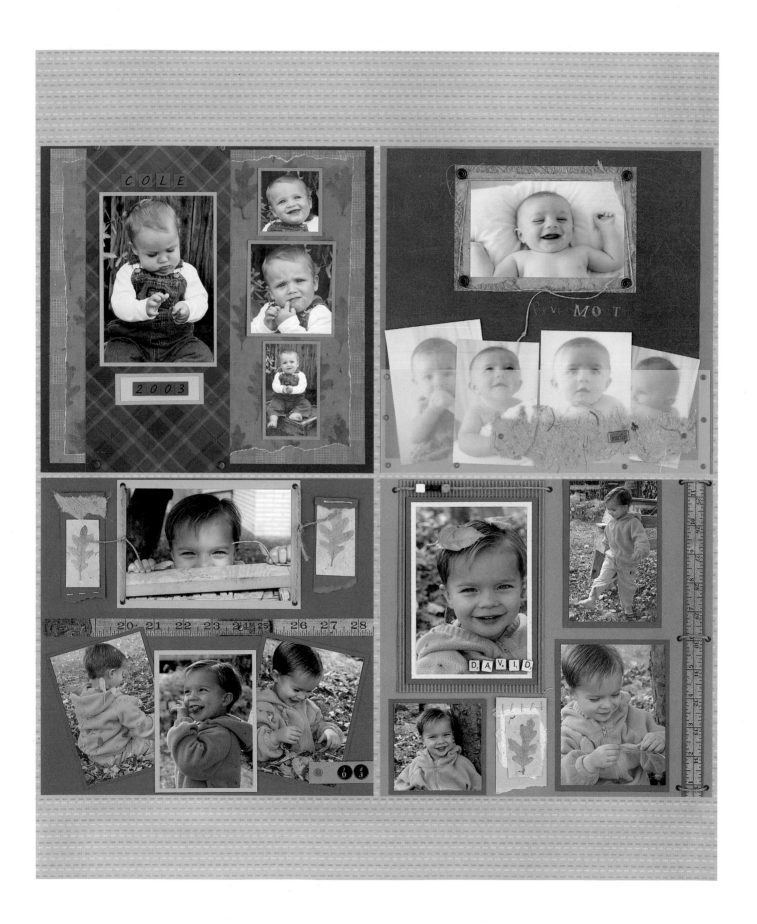

Scrapbooking Baby's Cherished Moments

200
Page
Designs

Rebecca Carter

Sterling Publication Co., Inc. New York

A Sterling/Chapelle Book

Chapelle, Ltd.:
Jo Packham
Sara Toliver
Cindy Stoeckl

Editors: Lana Hall and Melissa Maynard

Art Director: Karla Haberstich

Graphic Illustrator: Kim Taylor

Copy Editors: Anne Bruns, Marilyn Goff

Staff: Kelly Ashkettle, Areta Bingham, Donna Chambers, Emily Frandsen, Susan Jorgensen, Jennifer Luman, Barbara Milburn, Lecia Monsen, Linda Venditti, Desirée Wybrow,

Photography: Justin Buehler and Suzy Skadburg

Library of Congress Cataloging-in-Publication Data

Carter, Rebecca.
   Scrapbooking baby's cherished moments : 200 page designs / Rebecca Carter.
        p. cm.
   "A Sterling/Chapelle Book"
   Includes bibliographical references and index.
   ISBN 1-4027-0935-8
1. Photograph albums. 2. Photographs--Conservation and restoration. 3. Scrapbooks. 4. Baby books. I. Title.
TR465.C37273 2004
745.593--dc22

                          2004006110

10 9 8 7 6 5 4 3 2 1
Published by Sterling Publishing Co., Inc.
387 Park Avenue South, New York, NY 10016
©2004 by Rebecca Carter
Distributed in Canada by Sterling Publishing
c/o Manda Group, 165 Dufferin Street
Toronto, Ontario, Canada M6K 3H6
Distributed in Great Britain by Chrysalis Books Group PLC,
The Chrysalis Building, Bramley Road, London W10 6SP, England
Distributed in Australia by Capricorn Link (Australia) Pty. Ltd.,
P. O. Box 704, Windsor, NSW 2756, Australia
Printed and Bound in China

Sterling ISBN 1-4027-0935-8

If you have any questions or comments, please contact:
Chapelle, Ltd., Inc., P.O. Box 9252, Ogden, UT 84409
(801) 621-2777 • (801) 621-2788 Fax
e-mail: chapelle@chapelleltd.com
web site: www.chapelleltd.com

The copy, photographs, instructions, illustrations, and designs in this volume are intended for the personal use of the reader and may be reproduced for that purpose only. Any other use, especially commercial use, is forbidden under law without the written permission of the copyright holder.

Every effort has been made to ensure that all information in this book is accurate. However, due to differing conditions, tools, and individual skills, the publisher cannot be responsible for any injuries, losses, and/or other damages which may result from the use of the information in this book.

This volume is meant to stimulate craft ideas. If readers are unfamiliar or not proficient in a skill necessary to attempt a project, we urge that they refer to an instructional book specifically addressing the required technique.

Acknowledgments

Special thanks to my husband Rick, who did so much running around for me without complaint. He has supported me from the beginning—eighteen years ago.

To Michelle, who saved me with the use of her digital camera and the adjustment of photos at the last minute. Thank You!

To my four children, who put up with a mess for five weeks: Tyrel, my son who helped me with ideas when I became stumped, and especially Sophie, my six year old, who thought we wouldn't be able to put up the Christmas tree since the book would never be done.

In addition, thanks to all of the children in this book and to their mothers, who brought them into this world. Nothing is sweeter than what I see through the lens of my camera.

Photography used on the scrapbook pages (with the exception of those taken before I was born): Photo Art by Rebecca

Preface

I remember exactly where I was sitting in my sixth grade classroom when the teacher asked each of us what our favorite color was. I was so nervous to answer because I really didn't have a favorite color. I had so many reasons why I liked all of the colors. When it came to my turn to answer, I said I didn't have a favorite color but that I liked all of them. I had the same problem in college when I was doing my senior show for my art major. I took so many different art, weaving, sculpting, ceramic, and interior design classes that I didn't know which one I liked the most. One of my professors asked me why I didn't specialize in any one area and all I could answer was that I liked them all. I didn't have a specific desire to do any of them all the time. He thought that would hinder anything I did in the art field. I needed to pick an emphasis and stick with it. I obviously didn't listen. I do know that I took five semesters of weaving and was told that I could not take anymore. I needed to move on! I loved all of the nicely organized threads with their colors and textures.

It's obvious, a wide variety of styles and colors keep me interested. I jumped at the opportunity to do this book. Five years ago the medium of photography opened up to me. I could have never imagined I would be so inspired with my discovery. I was becoming quite "antsy" painting all of the time. This rejuvenated me in ways I never thought it could. The title on the book contract was *Scrapbooking Baby's Cherished Moments* and I was thrilled that I could use the infant photos I had done this year. Placing photographs in an album just wasn't enough. Paper craft is something I have always enjoyed, but haven't done anything with since my book *Scrapbooking for the First Time* was published four years ago. However, the market has changed so much. It was a real adventure to go to the scrapbook stores and see what was there. From there, I knew the hardware, fabric, and office supply stores would also offer some good ideas. Yes, maybe I went a little overboard with the things I found at the hardware store, but those little drawers have so many great things to offer.

My only advice is: Don't be afraid to use new things. Try a new color combination, but most importantly, enjoy what you are doing. Be adventurous by not limiting yourself to the same things. A saying I wrote for another publication that I try to live by is, "Life is an endless journey of opportunity. It is up to you what you do with it. Embrace it! In turn, it will give back to you in ways you may never have imagined." I hope you enjoy the variety of projects that I like to refer to as "individual pieces of art" that are offered in this book. I gave my heart and soul to every page and was sad when I knew I was almost done. I had so many more beautiful photographs that I would liked to have seen completed on a page that can be treasured forever. I tell people to take pictures even if you don't have time to put them in an album. At least you will have the photograph that will bring back a flood of memories. Enjoy!— *Rebecca*

Contents

General Instructions

Antiquing spray, using walnut ink crystals: This product is great for antiquing papers to give a little bit of a worn look. Simply mix the crystals with water and pour into a spray bottle. Refer to the instructions on the crystals. I used the spray several times, especially on the heritage pages and ripped edges of paper. I found that holding the paper at an angle and misting the edge worked the best. It dries quickly. It does wrinkle and bend the corners of the paper, but I like the effect. Placing it under a heavy object or an iron until it dries does help.

Beading needle: When using beads with very small openings, use a beading needle. Most of the beads in the scrapbooking sections have larger openings, but some may require beading needles. The needles are very thin and will bend easily when piercing paper. It does work so just be patient.

Craft wire: Tape the ends of the wire down in the back so it doesn't damage the page that it will rest against. Twisting the ends together will result in a "bulge" that will show on the front side.

Creative fonts: Be brave in using fonts and lettering. I am not a computer person, but you can find ways to make it work. Use a wide variety together to bring your page to life.

Differing paper widths: You may have already noticed that some 12"-square papers are not 12" square. Mixing different companies' papers together will give you uneven edges. I place two sides together, then trim the remaining two sides with a paper cutter.

Embossing aluminum foil: I used 24-gauge 1'x3' tooling foil, which is the thinnest weight available. Instructions for the use of the foil come with products. The thing you need to be most aware of is that the design is done on the back (matte) side, so everything is in reverse. For the lettering, first write the name or saying on a piece of vellum or tracing paper, turn the word over and place it on the back side of the aluminum. With a stylus, trace over the word. This will give you an imprint to work with. Now work on a softer surface, like a mat. Retrace your imprint. The more you trace it and the harder you press, the more the design will stand out on the front side. It is better to work on a slightly larger piece of aluminum, then cut it to the desired size.

Flower stitches: This is a lazy daisy stitch. I punched a small hole with a ¹⁄₁₆" punch where the center of the flower will be.

1. Tape the ribbon end down on the back.

2. Come up through the hole with the needle and ribbon. The petals are approximately ½" long from the center. Create a loop by going back down through the hole.

3. Lay the loop down on the paper and hold in place with your fingers.

4. Bring the needle up to the top of the loop and secure the loop into place. Do not pull tightly. Repeat with each petal.

5. Tape the ribbon end down when the flower is complete.

| Step: 2 | Step: 4 | Final petal |

Fray preventative: This is a must when using ribbons and laces to avoid fraying. Apply to cut ends and allow to dry before adhering to layouts.

General tools: Items that you will need to scrapbook include a pencil with an eraser, a ruler, and adhesives. There is a wide variety of scrapbooking adhesives on the market today. Be sure to read the adhesives' labels to make certain that it will not damage your photographs or paper. I love spray adhesives—especially for vellum. Just make certain you are placing it in the exact spot because removing it is difficult. Find a large flat box with high sides to spray in since spray adhesive can make a mess.

Lettering and keeping it straight: If straight is what you want, you will need a transparent ruler. I use one on every project I do. Measure where the lettering will be placed and leave the ruler there. Place the letters along the ruler's edge and adhere them. I found that placing the lettering crooked on purpose was much easier, but there are designs that must be straight. I always use a ruler with the alphabet snaps.

Vellums: Lay these flat to store. The large sheets of vellum with an embossed design on them can become very brittle. Be careful where you store them because the edges can easily tear and "break."

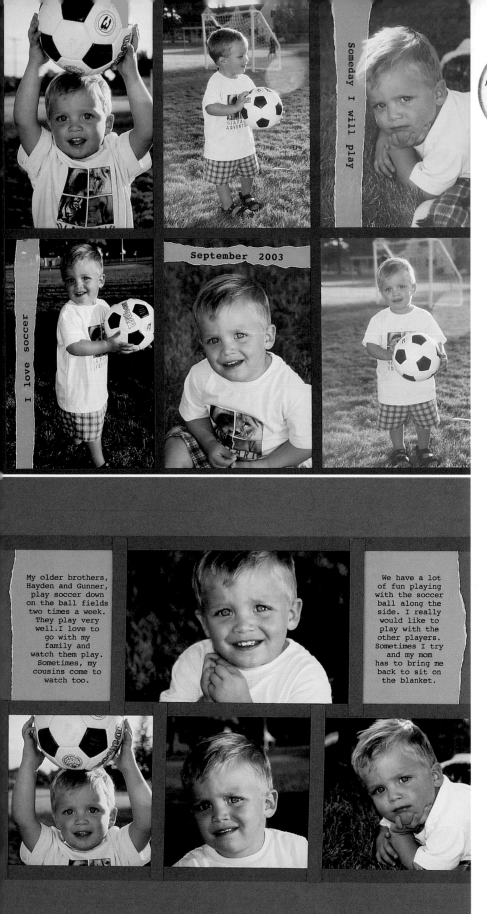

Tips on Photography

Photography is an art form and one of the most important elements in scrapbooking. Give important consideration to the photography and your scrapbook pages can be created more simply.

● **Add depth, variety, and practice**: Avoid flat-looking pictures by adding pointers to assist the eye. If the subject you are shooting is in the distance, add a tree or other objects in the foreground for depth perspective. Spice up your picture taking by adding variety to your shoots. Include landscapes, close-ups, vertical shots, wide angles, variety of weather conditions, and other different styles. Practice makes perfect, especially in photography. Take a variety of different shots of your subject and you are bound to get one you like.

● **Composition**: One of the most important elements in photography is composition. Ask yourself "What am I trying to capture, what reaction do I want the viewer to have?" Hold the camera steady when you shoot. Relax and use both hands while resting your elbows on your chest or other means of support.

● **Go vertical**: Many things look better in a vertical format, especially tall things such as the Empire State Building, Redwood trees, and children jumping into a puddle. So to emphasize height, go vertical.

● **Know your flash's range**: To avoid dark pictures, stay within the flash range of your camera. For many cameras, the maximum flash range is less than fifteen feet, which is about five steps away.

● **Make eye contact**: Pictures taken with direct eye contact will create a personal and inviting feeling that pulls the viewer into the picture. When taking a picture of a person, hold the camera at the person's eye level. For children, that means stooping down to their level or bringing them up to yours.

● **Move in close**: People make the most fascinating subjects so it is essential to capture their personality. Don't try to shoot the person's whole body, instead focus on their face, especially the eyes and mouth. Your goal is to fill the picture area with the subject you are photographing. However, avoid getting too close. Three feet (or about one step away) is the closest focusing point for most cameras.

● **Move subject from the middle**: Bring your picture to life by moving the subject off-center. Divide your viewfinder into a tic-tac-toe board and place your subject at one of the intersecting lines.

● **Put the sun behind you**: The standard for outdoor pictures has been to position yourself so the sun is behind you and to one side. Cloudy days are best for portraits. Practice photographing at dawn or in the late afternoon when the sun produces rich, warm colors and long shadows. Avoid shooting at noon when the sun provides harsh, "flat" lighting. Do not shoot very bright and very dark things together or you will lose all the detail and end up with over-exposed whites and underexposed darks.

● **Simplify the background**: A plain background frames the subject and makes them the focus of the picture. When you look through the viewfinder, make sure you observe the area surrounding your subject. Avoid having trees growing off the head of your subject.

● **Use flash outdoors**: Bright sun can create shadows, which you can eliminate by using your flash to lighten the face.

Steven Grant

Adventurous THINKER wants to fly Intrigued quiet

Photographing Infants and Children

● Producing beautiful photographs takes beautiful lighting. Avoid using direct light. Use a large window or a glass door. A porch with a large overhang makes a great studio.

● Avoid using the flash when photographing an infant. If you have good lighting, a flash is very seldom used.

● Use black-and-white film. It softens their beautiful skin.

● Use 3200 speed in really low lighting situations. It creates an old-fashioned feel. It was used for Delight on page 16 and Payton in Winter on page 25. Always try something new. You will be surprised with the outcome.

● First time? Try a very new infant that is asleep. It will be less frustrating for you. This is the easiest time to get the details of the eyelashes, hands, and feet. The younger the baby, the easier.

● Be patient. If you want to take good photographs, keep at it and it will come. With a great desire, comes great results.

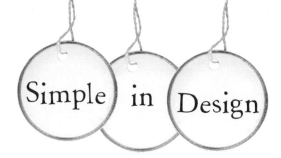

Simple in Design

The pages in this chapter are simple in layout, using a limited amount of color (usually solid) and not a large variety of product. The photographs tell the story and can stand on their own.

I hold your small LIFE in the palm of my HAND.

John Brent

MAIN PAPERS:

_BACKGROUND PAPER:
  textured teal
  cardstock

_LAYOUT PAPER:
  teal vellum

SUPPLIES:

_Adhesives

_Baby charms

_Clear scrapbook nails

_Lettering:
  computer-generated
  or handwritten

_Scraps of white vellum

_Thin white silk ribbon

John
Brent

Feb. 7
2003
7 lbs
5 oz.

DETAILS:

Emily is such a beautiful mother. I hoped to capture her pure joy of holding this child in her arms. ● Place a piece of cardstock behind the vellum. The scrapbook nails hold the vellum in place. ● Thread the ribbon through the charm and tie a knot ¾" away from the charm. Hang from the scrapbook nail.

Rachel Nicole

R

Ten Months

October '03

Rachel in the Basket

MAIN PAPERS:

_BACKGROUND PAPER:
  pink embossed
  cardstock

_LAYOUT PAPERS:
  light pink, cream
  cardstocks

SUPPLIES:

_Adhesives

_Beading needle

_Heart brads

_Lettering:
  computer-generated
  or handwritten

_Metal alphabet charm

_Silver beads

_Silver brads

_Silver metallic gel pen

–Tape

_Thread

_Tiny metal frame

DETAILS:

● Make a frame out of pink cardstock and attach it to the page with brads.
● Adhere all photographs. ● Carefully measure and mark the center of each photograph for the bead placement.
● Sew the beads on in one continuous thread. Tape over each hole as you go, this will protect the hole from ripping. Tape over the knot of the thread.

Little One

MAIN PAPERS:

_BACKGROUND PAPERS:
    textured cream,
    speckled tan,
    pale yellow cardstocks

_LAYOUT PAPER:
    white cardstock

SUPPLIES:

_Adhesives

_Scraps of white vellum

_Silver metallic gel pen

_Spray adhesive

DETAILS:

I started infant photography during the spring. This was one of them. What an opportunity to see a newborn and a mother's joy in holding her first child.
● The design was kept simple as not to take anything away from the photograph.
● Double-layer the vellum, giving it a slight border. Adhere the layers together with spray adhesive.

Little One

With your SWEET breath on my FACE I will hold you for FOREVER and a DAY and I will WATCH YOU sleep...

And know that you are MINE.

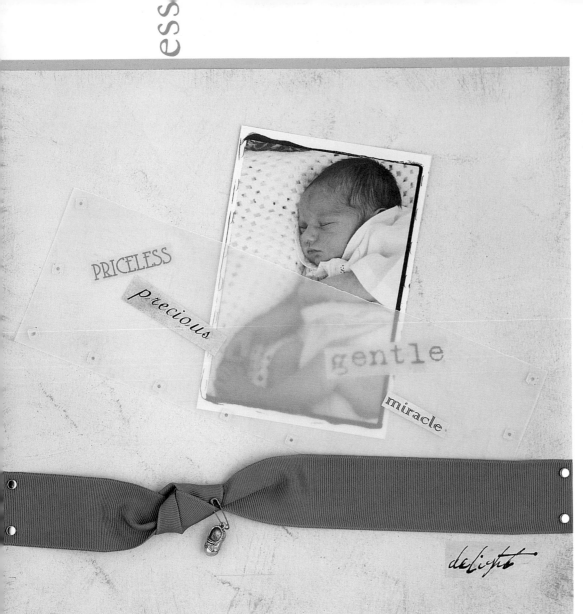

Delight

MAIN PAPERS:

_BACKGROUND PAPERS:
  light blue, tan
  cardstocks; textured
  scrapbook paper

SUPPLIES:

_1½"-wide blue grosgrain
  ribbon

_Adhesives

_Bootie charm

_Clear scrapbook nails

_Craft glue

_Fray preventative

_Safety pin

_Scraps of white vellum

_Silver brads

_Word stickers

DETAILS:

*This photograph spoke peace and quiet to
me and I wanted the layout to say the
same.* ● The ribbon measured
approximately 16" before tying the knot.
The knot is tied off center and adhered
with the brads. A little craft glue at both
ends makes it easier when applying the
brads. ● Hang the charm from the safety
pin that is attached to the knot. Place the
words on top and under the vellum.
Attach the vellum with the clear nails.
Attach the photograph inside the pocket.

Chubby Sleeping Baby

MAIN PAPERS:

_BACKGROUND PAPERS:
    white, pale yellow cardstocks

SUPPLIES:

_Adhesives

_Thin ribbon with word print

_Wave scissors

DETAILS:

● The words on the ribbon keep this layout simple and sweet. ● Trim and overlay the photographs.

tip

You can write your own message on the ribbon with a permanent or fabric marker; but be sure to not let the tip of the marker rest too long on the ribbon since this may make the ink bleed.

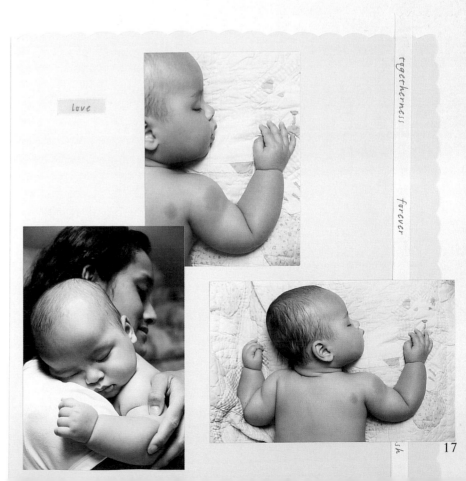

17

Triplets

December 12, 2002

hALEY

ICHOLAS

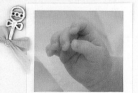

jILLIAN

Triplets

MAIN PAPERS:

_BACKGROUND PAPERS:
    cream, light green,
    light pink cardstocks

_LAYOUT PAPER:
    white cardstock

SUPPLIES:

_⅛" silk ribbons: blue, light green, pink

_Adhesives

_Alphabet stamps

_Baby charms

_Embroidery needle

_Ink pads: blue, green, pale pink

_Lettering:
    computer-generated
    or handwritten

_Scrapbook nails: green, pink

_Scraps of vellum: blue, pink, yellow

DETAILS:

My sister-in-law gave birth to three beautiful babies. All healthy, beautiful, and home by Christmas Eve. So blessed!
● Hang the charms by the silk ribbons.
● Make certain the names are lined up and spelled correctly.

Always Remember

MAIN PAPERS:

_BACKGROUND PAPERS:
light green cardstock;
textured light green
scrapbook paper

SUPPLIES:

_Adhesives

_Embroidery needle

_Lettering:
computer-generated
or handwritten

_Number snaps

_Rattle charm

_Scraps of vellum: pale
yellow, white

_Tape

_Thin ivory satin ribbon

_Tiny metal frame

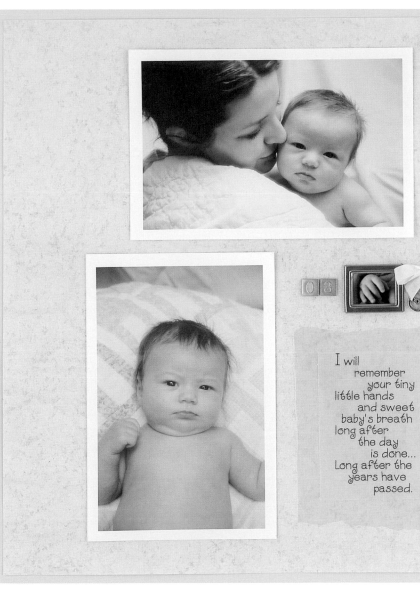

I will
remember
your tiny
little hands
and sweet
baby's breath
long after
the day
is done...
Long after the
years have
passed.

DETAILS:

*Payton was my first infant to
photograph. Such a beautiful baby.*
● Use a needle threaded with 8" of
ribbon to attach the ribbon and charm to
the background. Catch the charm opening
before sewing into the cardstock from the
front to the back. Cut off the ribbon in
the back. Two 4" pieces of ribbon will
remain with the charm on the front.
Secure the ends on the back side of the
paper with tape after tying them, in order
to keep the charm in place.

10 month old Rachel

Rachel and Her Brush

MAIN PAPERS:

_BACKGROUND PAPER:
    light green cardstock

_LAYOUT PAPERS:
    cream, pink cardstocks

SUPPLIES:

_Adhesives

_Assorted die-cut paper flowers

_Craft glue

_Silver metallic gel pen

DETAILS:

● Using craft glue, simply glue the flowers in place.

October 2003

tip

Don't worry about placing the flowers in an exact pattern—the more random the pattern, the more natural it will feel.

Trace in His Hat

MAIN PAPERS:

_BACKGROUND PAPERS:
   cream, tan cardstocks

_LAYOUT PAPERS:
   blue, blue-gray,
   cream, gray cardstocks

SUPPLIES:

_Adhesives

_Alphabet tiles

_Alphabet stamps

_Black elastic cord

_Black ink pad

_Brushed-silver eyelets

_Craft glue

_Number sticker

_Safety pin charm

_Silver jump ring

DETAILS:

● Randomly place the alphabet tiles onto the paper and glue them, with craft glue.
● A variety of letters and numbers adds to the square format of the layout. ● Hang the safety pin charm from the elastic with the jump ring.

Payton at Four Months

MAIN PAPERS:

_BACKGROUND PAPER:
  textured medium
  brown cardstock

_LAYOUT PAPERS:
  natural fiber, tan
  cardstocks

SUPPLIES:

_Adhesives

_Black elastic cord

_Gold eyelets

_Metal letters and numbers

DETAILS:

● This is a simple layout with easy embellishments. ● Thread the elastic through the eyelets and secure ends on back with tape.

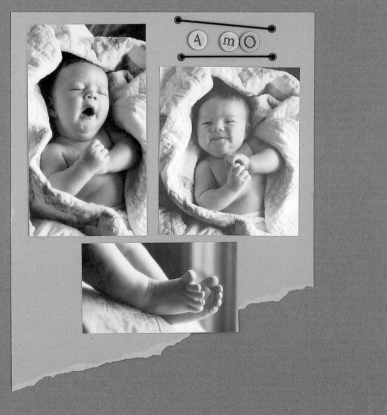

...the child

Let the Child Go...

MAIN PAPERS:

_BACKGROUND PAPER:
   textured black cardstock

_LAYOUT PAPER:
   white cardstock

SUPPLIES:

_Adhesives

_White opaque gel pen

DETAILS:

One of my favorite layouts. ● Keep it simple: white on black has huge impact. There is no need to add color in this layout.

he truly is...

let the child go...

...and he will discover

...the child he truly is.

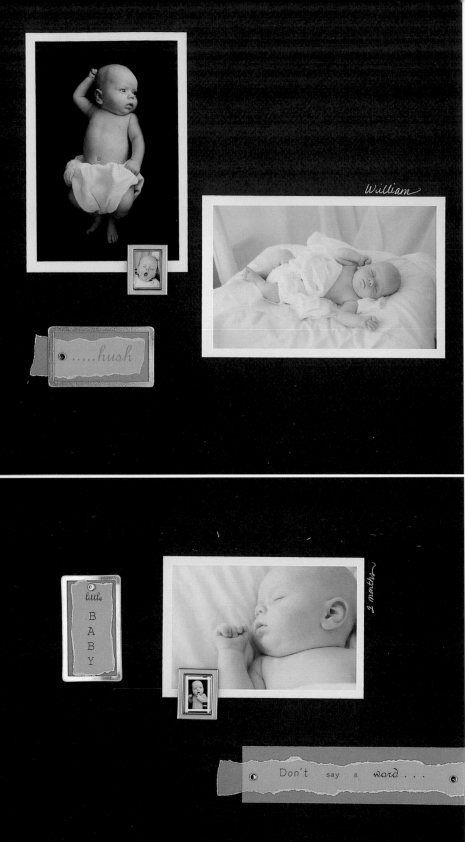

Hush, Little Baby

MAIN PAPERS:

_BACKGROUND PAPER:
   textured black cardstock

_LAYOUT PAPER:
   white vellum

SUPPLIES:

_Adhesives

_Lettering:
   computer-generated
   or handwritten

_Metal-edged labels (with vellum centers)

_Silver brads

_Silver metallic gel pen

_Tiny metal frames

DETAILS:

Again, I wanted a very simple page—I wanted to say the least amount with the largest effect. My sweet nephew.

● Choose a simple line from a song or phrase. Don't be afraid to separate the words between the two pages. It keeps your eyes moving.

tip

For the small picture frames, I used portions from the proof sheet enclosed with the developed photographs.

Payton in Winter

MAIN PAPERS:

_BACKGROUND PAPER:
   textured black cardstock

_LAYOUT PAPER:
   gray cardstock

SUPPLIES:

_Adhesives

_Black scrapbook nails

_Needle and thread

_Number snaps

_Scraps of white vellum

_Wire snowflakes

DETAILS:

● Attach the snowflakes onto the paper by stitching around each corner with a needle and thread. It only takes a couple of stitches to hold them in place.

...little baby

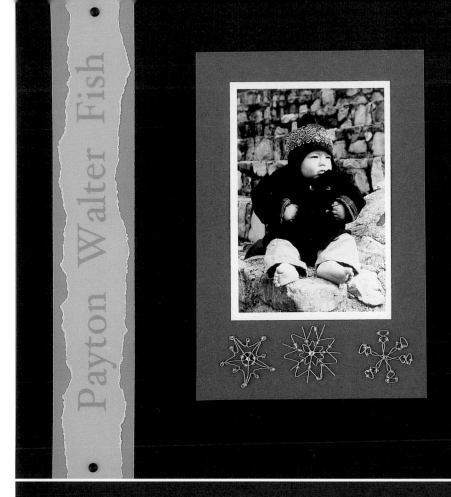

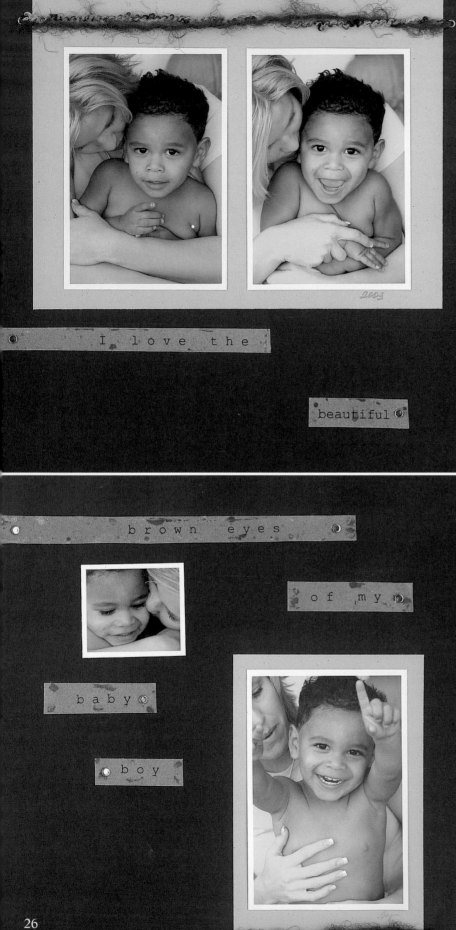

His Brown Eyes

MAIN PAPERS:

_BACKGROUND PAPER:
   dark brown cardstock

_LAYOUT PAPER:
   tan cardstock

SUPPLIES:

_Adhesives

_Bronze metallic gel pen

_Brown trims

_Craft glue

_Silver eyelets

_Tape

DETAILS:

I purposely wanted the craft glue to show through the vellum because it causes a watery effect. ● Thread the trim through the eyelets and secure on the back with tape.

tip

When applying the glue to the vellum, be sure to keep make it deliberate and clean or it may look like a mistake.

N.J.D

MAIN PAPERS:

_BACKGROUND PAPERS:
    dark blue, dark brown,
    sage green, tan cardstocks

SUPPLIES:

_Adhesives

_Assorted brads

_Assorted eyelets

_Jute

_Metal letters and numbers

_Number snaps

_Tape

_Wooden beads

DETAILS:

*My beautiful neighbor Nathan Jesse.
Sweetest child on the planet!*

● Create the backgrounds with strips of
colored cardstock. Overlap and secure
paper strips in place with eyelets. String
beads onto jute. Thread each end front to
back, then bring ends to front and knot.

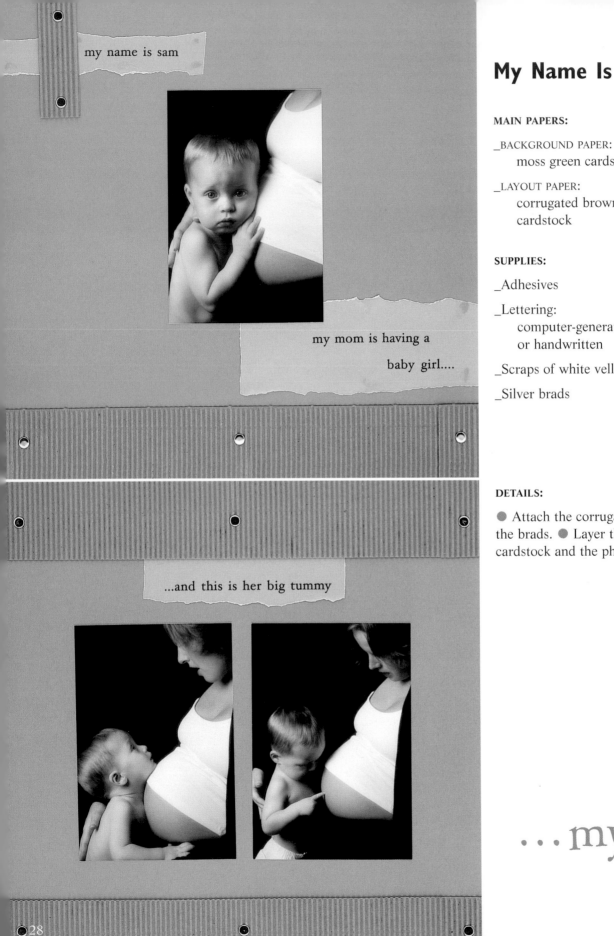

my name is sam

my mom is having a

baby girl....

...and this is her big tummy

My Name Is Sam

MAIN PAPERS:

_BACKGROUND PAPER:
moss green cardstock

_LAYOUT PAPER:
corrugated brown
cardstock

SUPPLIES:

_Adhesives

_Lettering:
computer-generated
or handwritten

_Scraps of white vellum

_Silver brads

DETAILS:

● Attach the corrugated cardstock with the brads. ● Layer the vellum under the cardstock and the photograph.

...my little

Tyler '03

MAIN PAPERS:

_BACKGROUND PAPER:
  speckled medium
  brown cardstock

_LAYOUT PAPERS:
  dark brown, cream,
  barn red cardstocks

SUPPLIES:

_⅛" hole punch

_Adhesives

_Gold brads

_Gold eyelets

_Jute

_Number snaps

DETAILS:

● Add a little color, such as the barn red cardstock, to highlight some of your favorite photographs.

sweetheart...

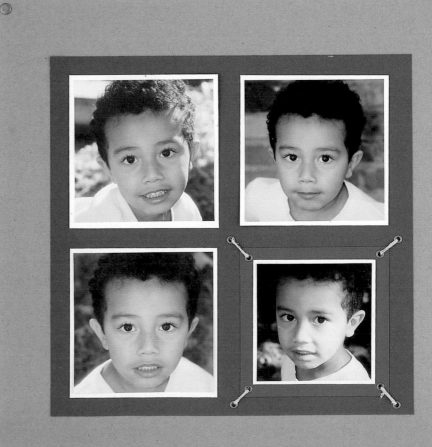

PRECIOUS (presh'-es) 1. of great worth 2. beloved; cherished

Giggle
a giddy laughter

Ty's Giggles

MAIN PAPERS:

_BACKGROUND PAPERS:
  dark blue, dark brown
  cardstocks

_LAYOUT PAPER:
  cream cardstock

SUPPLIES:

_Adhesives

_Antiqued defined word stickers

_Assorted brads

_Assorted metal-edged label
  (center removed)

_Black marker

_Metal letters

_Tiny metal frame

DETAILS:

● Cutting out the center of the metal label gave me a great little frame. ● Use brads for decoration.

T y

...such giddy

treasure (trezh'er) 1. accumulated wealth 2. something of great worth 3. irreplaceable; priceless

Brandon and the Hat

MAIN PAPERS:

_BACKGROUND PAPERS:
   smoky blue, cream
   cardstocks

_LAYOUT PAPERS:
   ivory, yellow cardstocks

SUPPLIES:

_⅛" hole punch

_Adhesives

_Brads: silver, yellow

_Lettering:
   computer-generated
   or handwritten

_Scraps of white vellum

DETAILS:

● Use the brads to hold the vellum into place. Use them, also, as accents to the entire page.

laughter...

Brandon is our beautiful
baby boy
with large blue eyes
a sweet
little
giggle....

blond curly hair
and a tiny
gap between

his two front

teeth.

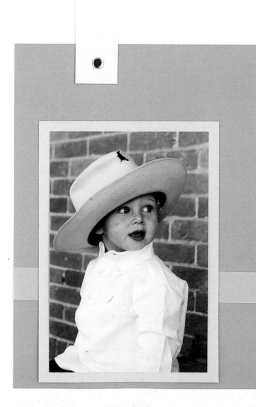

age two

Something Simple

MAIN PAPERS:

_BACKGROUND PAPER:
cream cardstock

_LAYOUT PAPERS:
cornflower blue, cream,
light sage green cardstocks

SUPPLIES:

_Adhesives

_Craft glue

_Green scrapbook nails

_Leaf skeletons

_Lettering:
computer-generated
or handwritten

_Scraps of white vellum

_Silver frames

_Tiny metal frames

DETAILS:

Alison loved these kittens, but they would rather have taken a nap. ● Overlay several pieces of cardstock. ● Adhere the leaf skeletons with craft glue.

how something this *Simple*…

…could be this *Special*.

Cole at Salem Pond

MAIN PAPERS:

_BACKGROUND PAPERS:
   navy blue, lime green
   cardstocks

_LAYOUT PAPERS:
   lime green, tan, white
   cardstocks

SUPPLIES:

_Adhesives

_Craft glue

_Lettering:
   computer-generated
   or handwritten

_Metal-edged label (center
   removed)

_Scraps of white vellum

_Silver alphabet stickers

_Silver brads

DETAILS:

● Adhere the frame around the
photograph with craft glue. ● Attach the
vellum with silver brads.

You Are a Marvel

MAIN PAPERS:

_BACKGROUND PAPER:
   light cornflower blue cardstock

_LAYOUT PAPERS:
   dark cornflower blue cardstock;
   white vellum

SUPPLIES:

_Adhesives

_Antiquing spray

_Clear scrapbook nails

_Lettering:
   computer-generated or handwritten

_Silver metallic gel pen

DETAILS:

Big blue eyes of my niece, Aspen.
● Choose one of your favorite sayings that best describes your child and repeat it in a square layout. ● Refer to General Instructions on page 8 for the antiquing spray. Use on the edges of the background cardstock.

Trey and Tyler

MAIN PAPERS:

_BACKGROUND PAPERS:
dark blue, lime green cardstocks

_LAYOUT PAPERS:
dark blue, light blue, cream, lime
green cardstocks

SUPPLIES:

_Adhesives

_Full-page cascading photograph
protector

_Full-page sectional photograph
protector

_Lettering:
computer-generated
or handwritten

_Scraps of white vellum

DETAILS:

● These page protectors have a series
of openings: one that is divided into
sections, and one that has a cascading
"waterfall" effect. Both are great for a lot
of photographs in one layout. ● Add a
little color behind the vellum to highlight
a word.

CHAPTER TWO

This chapter uses a few more products, experiments with combining patterns, and shows how to add a little creativity to show off the personality of the children being featured on each page.

Maddie Anne

MAIN PAPERS:

_BACKGROUND PAPERS:
  cream, pink
  cardstocks

SUPPLIES:

_⅛" hole punch

_¼"-wide pink satin ribbon

_Adhesives

_Alphabet snaps

_Assorted buttons

_Ruler

_Silver metallic gel pen

_Tape

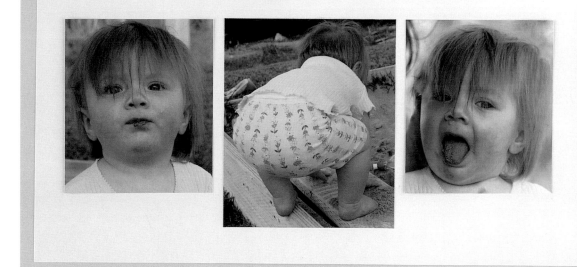

DETAILS:

● Cut small slits into the cream cardstock to slide the ribbon through. Place a piece of tape over the ribbon in the back so it won't slide. ● Use the ruler to create a line for the alphabet snaps. Mark off the center of the snap. Punch holes. Erase marks before snapping the letters into place.

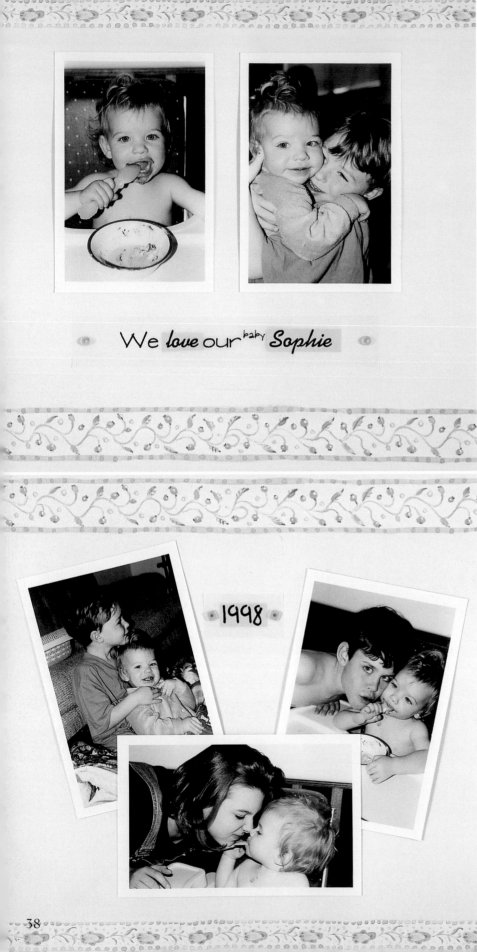

We love our baby Sophie

1998

Our Baby Sophie

MAIN PAPERS:

_BACKGROUND PAPERS:
   pale blue, pale green
   cardstocks

SUPPLIES:

_Adhesives

_Lettering:
   computer-generated
   or handwritten

_Paper border stickers

_Scrapbook nails: pink, yellow

_Scraps: green, pink cardstock;
   white vellum

DETAILS:

*My blue-eyed spunky baby girl is adored
by her siblings.* ● Design with simple
paper borders, which are not a lot of
work. ● Place the colored cardstock
behind the vellum to highlight the words.

Sophie, Sophie

MAIN PAPERS:

_BACKGROUND PAPERS:
   blue, green cardstocks

_LAYOUT PAPERS:
   light blue, cream,
   tan cardstocks

SUPPLIES:

_¼"-wide tan grosgrain ribbon

_24-gauge craft wire

_Adhesives

_Alphabet stamps

_Assorted beads

_Assorted buttons

_Assorted ink pads

_Clear glass stone

_Craft glue

_Fray preventative

_Metal-edged label (center removed)

_Needle and thread

_Needle-nosed pliers

_Silver brads

_Silver eyelets

_String

_White elastic cord

_Wire cutters

DETAILS:

● Create bends in the wires by shaping with needle-nosed pliers. Curl one end, add beads. Curl other end to keep beads in place. ● Sting the buttons and glue to the paper.

Emma Marie

March 2000

Emma's Nursery

MAIN PAPERS:

_BACKGROUND PAPER:
  tan cardstock

_LAYOUT PAPERS:
  blue, green, pink,
  white cardstocks

SUPPLIES:

_Adhesives

_Color copies from a nursery
  rhyme book (ripped edges)

_Craft glue

_Decorative buttons

_Lettering:
  computer-generated
  or handwritten

_Pink brads

_Scraps of white vellum

DETAILS:

I felt the nursery rhyme pictures competed with the photographs, so I veiled them with a piece of vellum, cut slightly narrower. ● Attach all the buttons with craft glue.

...she is such

Piglet

MAIN PAPERS:

_BACKGROUND PAPERS:
   textured pink cardstock;
   speckled cream, pink polk-a-dot
   scrapbook papers

_LAYOUT PAPERS:
   textured pink,
   cream cardstocks

Supplies:

_Adhesives

_Assorted beads

_Assorted pink buttons

_Lettering:
   computer-generated
   or handwritten

_Linen jute

_Tape

Details:

Rachel wanted absolutely nothing to do with this costume! ● String the beads through the buttonholes. ● Secure the knotted ends of the jute down in the back with tape to avoid them coming loose.

a character

Rachel and the Piglet Costume

Meikel Rene

October 2003

meow!

Meow

MAIN PAPERS:

_BACKGROUND PAPERS:
    textured pink,
    tan cardstocks

_LAYOUT PAPER:
    cream cardstock

SUPPLIES:

_1/16"-wide pink grosgrain ribbon

_1/8" hole punch

_Adhesives

_Embroidering needle

_Lettering:
    computer-generated
    or handwritten

_Pink brads

_Scraps of white vellum

_Silver charms: cats, flowers

Mommy and I went on a walk...

I saw a kitty across the street...

I wanted to hold that kitty...

But the kitty didn't want to hold me.

DETAILS:

● First create a hole, then attach the flowers with brads. ● Sew the charms into place with pink grosgrain ribbon.

tip

To avoid any lumps, secure the ribbon edges down with tape instead of knotting them.

Meikel's Sweater

MAIN PAPERS:

_BACKGROUND PAPERS:
    cream, green, lavender
    cardstocks

_LAYOUT PAPER:
    light blue cardstock

SUPPLIES:

_Adhesives

_Assorted beads

_Assorted ribbon trims

_Clear bubble letters and numbers

_Head pins

_Needle and thread

_Scraps of white vellum

_Silver eyelets

_Tape

DETAILS:

● Create a pattern for the ribbon. Carefully measure the placements for the eyelets so they are the same on both sides. Then thread ribbon so it is straight. Add a few beads randomly on the ribbons. Sew on the beads around the name. ● Secure the ends of the ribbons on the back with tape instead of tying knots. Use tape to flatten down some of the trims when placing photographs.

Meikel's Car

MAIN PAPERS:

_BACKGROUND PAPER:
  light sage green cardstock

_LAYOUT PAPERS:
  light blue-green,
  textured pink cardstocks

SUPPLIES:

_⅛" hole punch

_Adhesives

_Double-sided tape

_Letter and number snaps

_Letter stickers

_Metal-edged circular labels

_Silver eyelets

_Silver jump rings

_Tape

_Unique trims

DETAILS:

● Lace the trims through the eyelets and secure to the back with tape. ● Hang the labels from the trim with jump rings, then secure with double-sided tape.

Meikel and Mommy

MAIN PAPERS:

_BACKGROUND PAPERS:
  sage green, textured pink cardstocks;
  plaid scrapbook paper

_LAYOUT PAPERS:
  cream, pink plaid
  scrapbook papers

SUPPLIES:

_⅜" hole punch

_½"-wide pink grosgrain ribbon

_Adhesives

_Embroidery needle

_Fray preventative

_Lettering:
  computer-generated
  or handwritten

_Lime green brads

_Scraps of white vellum

_Tape

DETAILS:

● After adhering the photographs and vellum, mark the placement for each flower. Punch holes on the markings. The ⅜" hole punch seems large. However, this is needed to make a hole large enough for the grosgrain ribbon to fit through. Create the flowers by threading the ribbon through the punched hole and wrap it twice around the needle. Thread the needle back through the punched hole. Cut the end of the ribbon and tie a knot on the back of the page. Secure the knot with tape. Repeat with the remaining flowers.

I love to spend time with my mommy. My favorite place to play is in the front yard of my grandparents house in Salem. There are a lot of things to do there. It is a big farm with a lot of animals and trees to climb. My favorite thing to do is to play with my mommy. I laugh when she tickles me. I laugh the most when she tickles me under my arms. I like to play "where's mommies tongue".

October 2003

45

Meikel's Flowers

MAIN PAPERS:

_BACKGROUND PAPER:
   textured bright orange linen
   scrapbook paper

_LAYOUT PAPERS:
   light sage green,
   white, light yellow cardstocks

SUPPLIES:

_⅛" hole punch

_Adhesives

_Assorted beads

_Assorted die-cut paper flowers

_Assorted ribbon trims

_Beading needle and thread

_Green embroidery floss

_Silver eyelets

_Silver metallic gel pen

DETAILS:

There is a variety of accessories on the market to use to embellish any page. These delicate little flowers can add such an impact with very little effort. All the work is done for you. ● The beading on the page is for decoration, but adds a fun dimension to each page. ● The stitching for the flower stems and the outside edges of the leaves is a simple straight stitch. Fill in the leaves with a lazy daisy stitch (refer to General Instructions page 9 for instructions on the Flower Stitches). Use a pencil to lightly mark where you want each flower before stitching. Make certain it is light enough that it doesn't show once the flower stem is stitched.

Remi

MAIN PAPERS:

_BACKGROUND PAPERS:
> green floral,
> burnt orange cardstocks

_LAYOUT PAPER:
> light green cardstock

SUPPLIES:

_¼"-wide green grosgrain ribbon

_Adhesives

_Alphabet snaps

_Assorted beads

_Awl

_Bead glue

_Craft glue

_Linen jute

_Metal flower eyelet

_Needle and thread

_Silver eyelets and brads

_Tape

DETAILS:

● Simply rip the green cardstock along the edges. ● String the beads with thread along the folded edge of the photographs and attach about every 2"–3". ● On the back side, make certain to tape the ribbons over the knots so they do not rub loose. ● Sew all of the beads randomly around the page. ● First adhere the beads to the flower eyelet with craft glue, then attach the flower to the page with the brad. ● Make the holes in the ribbon for the alphabet snaps with an awl.

Best Friends

MAIN PAPERS:

_BACKGROUND PAPER:
  speckled tan cardstock

_LAYOUT PAPERS:
  green, burnt orange,
  barn red cardstocks

SUPPLIES:

_⅛" hole punch

_³⁄₁₆"-wide light green silk ribbon

_½"-wide green grosgrain ribbon

_Adhesives

_Alphabet stamps

_Assorted beads

_Awl

_Bead glue

_Butterfly embellishment

_Colored brads

_Craft glue

_Green ink pad

_Needle and thread

_Silver flower charms

_Zigzag scissors
  (optional: replace with rickrack)

DETAILS:

● Using an awl, make holes for the brads.
● With brads, attach the grosgrain ribbon to the bottom of the page. ● Using the silk ribbon, hand-stitch the flower leaves.
● Create the flower stem with zigzag scissors. Attach the flowers before the beads. First, work with each flower petal individually. (The craft glue dries too quickly to apply glue to the whole flower.)
● Allow project to dry for several hours before putting it into a page protector.

Jordon's Daisies

MAIN PAPERS:

_BACKGROUND PAPERS:
  light green cardstock; embossed
  daisies scrapbook paper

SUPPLIES:

_⅜"-wide green grosgrain ribbon

_Adhesives

_Assorted beads

_Assorted charms

_Awl

_Bead glue

_Fray preventative

_Lettering:
  computer-generated
  or handwritten

_Metal letter charms

_Needle and thread

_Scraps of white vellum

_Silver eyelets

_Tiny metal frame

DETAILS:

● Before attaching the metal charm
letters, punch holes for their placement on
the green ribbon with an awl, after the
ribbon is placed on the paper. ● Stitch
the charms to hang from the ribbon. ●
Tear out the center of one sheet of daisy
scrapbook paper to make a picture frame.
● Using bead glue, adhere the beads to
the middle of the flower eyelets. Make
certain the beads are dry before sliding
the pages into a page protector.

You only gave
me a smile,
My name you
did not call,
And yet it
made my day
The Brightest
Day of all.
You only gave
me a smile,
My name you
did not call,
And yet it
made my day
The Brightest
Day of all.

Perry Tanksley

Jordon just turned three.
We went up to the River Woods
to have our
family photos for the year.
She looked so cute dressed up
in her hat and she loved
the daisies.

Mommy's Angel

MAIN PAPERS:

_BACKGROUND PAPERS:
  green, tan cardstocks

_LAYOUT PAPER:
  white embossed floral vellum

SUPPLIES:

_Adhesives

_Aluminum foil

_Craft glue

_Lettering:
  computer-generated
  or handwritten

_Scraps of white vellum

_Spray adhesive

DETAILS:

I was inspired by a frame with glass edging. ● Adhere the photographs to the paper. The aluminum foil works great as an edging around photographs and paper. ● Create strips of foil with folded edges. Use an old pair of scissors when making mitered edges with the foil because the foil will dull them. ● Measure each section of paper around the photograph. Cut the vellum to fit the pieces. Use spray adhesive to apply the vellum. Glue a strip of folded aluminum foil leading from each photograph corner to the corner of the paper. ● Glue strips of the foil around the photographs and paper.

Angel and Gracin

MAIN PAPERS:

_BACKGROUND PAPER:
   dark brown
   cardstock

SUPPLIES:

_⅜"-wide pink silk ribbon

_Acrylic letters

_Adhesives

_Clear beads

_Needle and thread

_Scraps of white vellum

_Silver metallic gel pen

_Spray adhesive

DETAILS:

When I placed the acrylic letters onto the brown paper, the letters disappeared.
● Place the vellum behind the letters making them readable. To put a little texture behind the letters, I intentionally place some of the letters along the ripped edge of the vellum. Adhere the letters to the background paper with spray adhesive.
● Refer to General Instructions on page 9 for the Lazy Daisy Stitch. Don't pull the ribbon tight when making the petals. Sew three beads into each flower center.

51

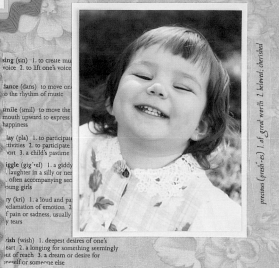

April 2000

Morgan is my miracle angel that was sent to me for a special purpose. I believe she is my guardian angel to help me through all of my earthly trials. She is a beautiful child with a very special quiet spirit to guide me every day. I smile each time I look at her sweet smile that reminds me there is just a little bit of heaven here on earth.

Miracle Angel

MAIN PAPERS:

_BACKGROUND PAPERS:
    tan cardstock;
    assorted floral scrapbook papers

_LAYOUT PAPERS:
    cream, sage green,
    tan cardstocks

SUPPLIES:

_Adhesives

_Antiqued defined word stickers

_Assorted beads

_Assorted rickrack

_Fray preventative

_Head pins

_Heart charms

_Scraps of white vellum

_Spray adhesive

DETAILS:

● Use a piece of cardstock as a base.
● Cut and adhere the assorted floral paper into interesting shapes. ● Use the rickrack to cover the seams of the paper.
● Copy the defined word stickers onto the vellum and adhere with spray adhesive.

Zachary and Morgan

MAIN PAPERS:

_BACKGROUND PAPERS:
    brown, green cardstocks;
    plaid, stripe scrapbook papers

_LAYOUT PAPERS:
    cream, dark moss
    green, tan cardstocks

SUPPLIES:

_24-gauge craft wire

_Adhesives

_Aluminum foil

_Lettering:
    computer-generated
    or handwritten

_Metal alphabet charms

_Metal mesh

_Needle and thread

_Scraps of vellum: floral, white

_Silver brads and eyelets

_Stylus

_Tape

DETAILS:

● Hold the mesh into place with the eyelet and wire, but first make a hole with a needle for the wire to thread through. Secure the ends of the wire on the back side with tape. ● Make the frames with strips of the aluminum foil. ● Refer to General Instructions page 8 for embossing the lettering on the aluminum foil.

Shabby Chic Morgan

MAIN PAPERS:

_BACKGROUND PAPERS:
   cream cardstock;
   floral scrapbook paper

SUPPLIES:

_24-gauge silver craft wire

–Adhesives

_Alphabet stamps

_Assorted beads

_Assorted buttons

_Assorted ribbons, rickracks, trims

_Craft glue

_Fabric scraps

_Green scrapbook nails

_Ink pads: brown, green, red

_Letter stickers

_Lettering:
   computer-generated
   or handwritten

_Metal-edged label

_Needle and thread

_Scraps of white vellum

_Sewing machine

DETAILS:

● Cover the fabric loosely with vellum because the prints are a little heavy in color. Machine-stitch them onto the fabrics. ● Sew the beads on by hand. ● Adhere the buttons and rickrack with craft glue.

Angel

MAIN PAPERS:

_BACKGROUND PAPERS:
 tan cardstock;
 cream floral, lavender
 floral, pink stripe
 scrapbook papers

_LAYOUT PAPERS:
 cream, light sage green
 cardstocks

SUPPLIES:

_Adhesives

_Antiqued defined word
 stickers

_Fabric trim

_Fray preventative

_Lettering:
 computer-generated
 or handwritten

_Pink brads

_Scraps of white vellum

_Sewing machine

_Spray adhesive

_Tan photo corners

DETAILS:

● Use a full piece of cardstock as your base for the strips of paper to create the background. ● Copy the words from the stickers onto vellum. Cut and tear apart. Use spray adhesive to adhere the vellum randomly along the bottom. ● Optional: machine stitch the trim.

Abigail in Silver Frame

MAIN PAPERS:

_BACKGROUND PAPERS:
  moss green cardstock;
  floral scrapbook paper

_LAYOUT PAPER:
  pale blue
  scrapbook paper

SUPPLIES:

_Adhesives

_Aluminum foil

_Double-sided tape

_Floral design pattern

_Silver buttons
  (backs cut off)

_Stylus

DETAILS:

● Refer to General Instructions on page 8 for embossing aluminum foil. ● To frame a 4"x6" print, measure a 5½"x8" piece of aluminum foil. Adjustments will need to be made in the design on the frame to accommodate the corners and the size of the photograph. Secure the frame with double-sided tape. Be careful to position the frame exactly. (It is very difficult to move once the tape has touched the background paper.)

Cookies for Breakfast

MAIN PAPERS:

_BACKGROUND PAPERS:
 textured natural green, pastel tile,
 textured pink cardstocks

_LAYOUT PAPER:
 natural cream cardstock

SUPPLIES:

_½"-wide pink lace trim

_1"-wide lace trim

_Adhesives

_Assorted beads

_Assorted buttons

_Assorted trims

_Beading needle

_Border stickers

_Brown shipping tag

_Craft glue

_Lettering:
 computer-generated
 or handwritten

_Linen thread

_Ribbon flower

_Scraps of white vellum

_Spray adhesive

DETAILS:

My niece who is never short on sugar!
● Adhere the textured natural green
paper with craft glue. ● Use spray
adhesive to adhere the vellum. ● Adhere
buttons onto the page with craft glue.

59

CHAPTER THREE

There is something about the past and the things of that time which intrigue me. I covet old photographs filled with their richness of a different era. Don't be afraid to take apart old damaged hats and create something useful and new. I discovered hat labels are a great addition to pages.

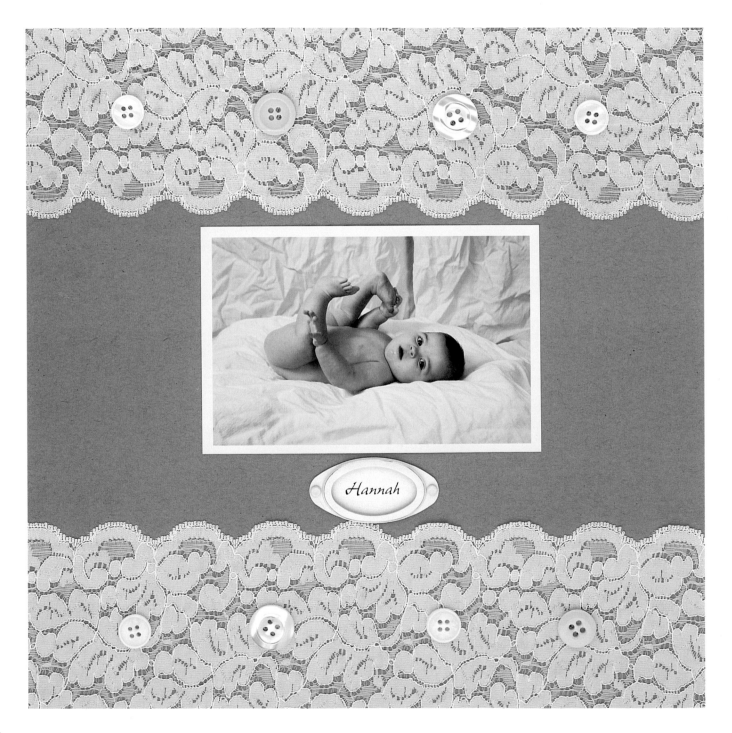

Hannah

Buttons and Lace

MAIN PAPERS:

_BACKGROUND PAPER:
    speckled tan cardstock

_LAYOUT PAPER:
    cream cardstock

SUPPLIES:

_4"-wide cream lace

_Adhesives

_Assorted buttons

_Craft glue

_Cream metal label frame

_Lettering:
    computer-generated
    or handwritten

_Silver metallic gel pen

_Spray adhesive

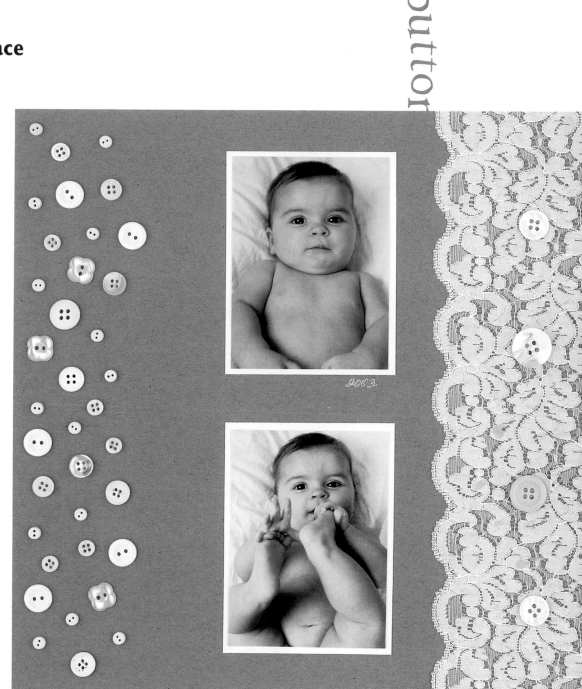

DETAILS:

She could be a model! ● Adhere the lace with spray adhesive. ● With craft glue, adhere buttons into place. ● Write important information, such as dates, onto the background paper with gel pen.

Becoming a Mother

MAIN PAPERS:

_BACKGROUND PAPERS:
  tan cardstock;
  floral, musical score vellums

_LAYOUT PAPER:
  tan cardstock

SUPPLIES:

_3"-wide tan lace

_Adhesives

_Antiqued-gold buttons (backs cut off)

_Assorted ribbon trims

_Beads

_Craft glue

_Heart paperclips

_Mini buttons

_Needle and thread

_Spray adhesive

DETAILS:

My uncle brought these photographs over from Germany of his wife and their firstborn daughter. They were breathtaking to me and I wanted to frame them immediately. ● Adhere the vellum and flat lace with spray adhesive. ● Adhere the mini buttons on with craft glue. ● Sew the hearts and beads onto the page.

Norma Jean

MAIN PAPERS:

_BACKGROUND PAPERS:
  brown cardstock;
  musical score, rose
  vellums

SUPPLIES:

_½"-wide gold sheer ribbon

_5"-wide cream lace

_Adhesives

_Assorted beads

_Needle and thread

_Ribbon buckles

_Spray adhesive

_Tiny metal frame

DETAILS:

This page contains one of my favorite photographs of my mother as a child.
● Place the background papers behind the vellum to add color. It will give it a whole different look. The darker the cardstock, the more subtle the vellum design becomes. Adhere the vellum to the cardstock with spray adhesive. ● Use spray adhesive to adhere the lace.

My Dad

MAIN PAPERS:

_BACKGROUND PAPERS:
cream script, leaf
pattern, textured
purple scrapbook
papers

_LAYOUT PAPERS:
textured black, cream
cardstocks

SUPPLIES:

_³⁄₁₆"-wide black
flocked ribbon

_1"-wide gold grosgrain
ribbon

_Adhesives

_Assorted buttons

_Black fine-tipped marker

_Border stickers

_Deckle-edged scissors

_Fray preventative

_Small oval stickers

_Tiny metal frame

DETAILS:

This is my father in Germany. ● Use
a piece of cardstock as your base for
layering the strips of paper to create the
background. ● Use fray preventative
on all ribbon edges.

Mom and Her Siblings

MAIN PAPERS:

_BACKGROUND PAPERS:
   cream script, embossed paisley,
   textured dark purple lace scrapbook
   papers

_LAYOUT PAPERS:
   black, dark brown, cream
   cardstocks

SUPPLIES:

_1½"-wide gold sheer ribbon

_Adhesives

_Antiquing spray

_Assorted beaded ribbon trims

_Assorted beads

_Beading needle

_Black flocked ribbon

_Flat-sided pearls

_Floral stickers

_Fray preventative

_Green scrapbook nails

_Head pins

_Lettering:
   computer-generated
   or handwritten

_Needle and thread

_Ribbon buckle

_Tape

DETAILS:

● String the beads on head pins, bend
ends to create a loop, and hook to the
beaded trim. (The beads on the top page
were stitched right to the paper with the
needle and thread.) Secure the knots on
the back with tape.

My mother, Norma
and her siblings
Marion and Roland
1930's

Emma the Cherub

MAIN PAPERS:

_BACKGROUND PAPERS: tan cardstock; floral scrapbook paper

_LAYOUT PAPERS: scraps of cream, rose, tan cardstocks

SUPPLIES:

_½"-wide antique lace

_1"-wide tan grosgrain ribbon

_5½"-wide antique lace

_Adhesives

_Buttons (backs cut off)

_Craft glue

_Lettering: computer-generated or handwritten

_Metal label frame

_Safety pin

_Spray adhesive

_Tiny metal frames

DETAILS:

Emma is my good friend's daughter. She has rolls from head to toe. Cherub was the first word that came to me when I used this photograph for the layout. ● Adhere the 5½"-wide lace with spray adhesive. ● Frame the main photograph with the ½"-wide antique lace and then back with cardstock. ● The bow is held on with a safety pin though the back. ● Adhere the buttons with craft glue. ● Adhere the 5½"-wide lace, above the two photographs, on the back in an arch. Save the bottom as you may use it on the future project.

My Father's Father

MAIN PAPERS:

_BACKGROUND PAPERS: tan cardstock; assorted print scrapbook papers

_LAYOUT PAPER: tan cardstock

SUPPLIES:

_Adhesives

_Antiquing spray

_Assorted ribbon trims

_Brown cord

_Buttons (backs cut off)

_Craft glue

_Fray preventative

_Lettering: computer-generated or handwritten

_Metal label frames

_Ribbon buckle

DETAILS:

These priceless photographs of my father and grandfather in Germany were only 1½" square. I had them enlarged digitally, which was an excellent idea for such a great project. ● Use the tan cardstock as the base for the strips of papers. ● Cover the edges of the papers with the ribbon trims. All ribbon ends need fray preventative. ● Be very careful not to use too much glue when adhering the cord. Apply a small amount of glue to the ends of the cord to prevent fraying.

When a CHILD is born, so is a Grandparent

A Grandparent is Born

MAIN PAPERS:

_BACKGROUND PAPERS: tan cardstock; fleur-de-lis patterned, tan script, travel patterned scrapbook papers

_LAYOUT PAPER: light green cardstock

SUPPLIES:

_⅝"-wide pale smoky blue grosgrain ribbon

_2"-wide cream lace

_3"-wide gold satin ribbon

_Adhesives

_Antiquing spray

_Assorted beads

_Assorted buttons

_Fray preventative

_Needle and thread

_Ribbon buckle

DETAILS:

● Refer to General Instructions on page 8 for antiquing spray. Apply it on the ripped edges of paper since they are a little too white. ● String the wide ribbon through the ribbon buckle. The ends of the ribbon tuck behind the buckle, making the loops of the bow. Sew the ribbon ends together and adhere the bow to the background paper. To flatten the bow, place something heavy on top and allow time to dry. ● Sew the beads to each side of the quote.

Sophia

MAIN PAPERS:

_BACKGROUND PAPERS:
   green, plum, sage cardstocks;
   embossed plum, cream script,
   dark tan scrapbook papers;
   embossed tan floral vellum

_LAYOUT PAPERS:
   cream, plum, light speckled tan
   cardstocks

SUPPLIES:

_½"-wide beaded ribbon trim

_1"-wide cream lace

_1"-wide cream sheer ribbon

_Adhesives

_Assorted beads

_Black cord

_Craft glue

_Embossed floral border stickers

_Fray preventative

_Jewels

_Lettering:
   computer-generated
   or handwritten

_Metal label frame

_Needle and thread

_Pressed flower

_Ribbon buckle

DETAILS:

● Use a piece of cardstock for the base to place the strips of embossed and printed paper. ● To make the tag, adhere the pressed flower with craft glue to a rectangular cardstock. Sew the beads into place on each end. ● Glue the lace behind the photo for design.

69

Mommy and Daddy's Notes

MAIN PAPERS:

_BACKGROUND PAPERS:
    floral, green paisley
    scrapbook papers

_LAYOUT PAPER:
    mossy green
    scrapbook paper

SUPPLIES:

_Adhesives

_Assorted laces and
    ribbons

_Border stickers

_Clear beads

_Deckle-edged scissors

_Fray preventative

_Lettering:
    computer-generated
    or handwritten

_Metal-edged label
    (centers removed)

_Needle and thread

_Pearl beads

_Ribbon buckles

_Velcro dots

DETAILS:

● Adhere strips of printed paper to a piece of cardstock. ● The notes are folded cardstock with a deckle edge on the flap. Notes from mom and dad, or even grandma and grandpa, are great.
● The beads are sewn onto the ribbon.
● Weave the buckles on before the beads.
● Close the note cards with velcro dots.

entering my

…little girl

Mommy

Daddy

I've never had a little girl of my own before. You have filled my every wish. Each time I hold you, you remind me of your mother, with your dark brown hair and beautiful light skin. Thank you for coming into my life.

tip

Add a Velcro dot to close the folded note to make the scrapbook page more interactive.

Sweet Memories of Morgan

MAIN PAPERS:

_BACKGROUND PAPERS:
  pale smoky blue
  cardstock;
  embossed floral vellum

_LAYOUT PAPERS:
  cream, sage green,
  tan cardstocks;
  musical score, cream
  script scrapbook
  papers

SUPPLIES:

_⅝"-wide cream grosgrain
  ribbon

_Adhesives

_Alphabet, border,
  flower stickers

_Antiquing spray

_Assorted beads

_Assorted buttons

_Assorted lace trims

_Brown shipping label

_Craft glue

_Fray preventative

_Gold brads

_Gold metallic gel pen

_Head pins

_Heart paperclips

_Spray adhesive

DETAILS:

● Use fray preventative on all cut ribbon ends. ● Use spray adhesive to attach the lace to the background cardstock. ● Refer to General Instructions on page 8 for the antiquing spray. Use it to age the edges of the label, the border around the photograph, and the edge of layout sheet. Spray these individually before assembling. ● Adhere the lace above the photograph into an arch with craft glue.

sweet memories

Sophie's Garden

MAIN PAPERS:

_BACKGROUND PAPERS:
    golden cardstock;
    floral, embossed leaf
    scrapbook paper

_LAYOUT PAPERS:
    blue, cream, dark purple,
    medium purple cardstocks;
    white vellum

SUPPLIES:

_⅜"-wide cream lace

_Adhesives

_Antiqued defined words

_Antiquing spray

_Assorted beads

_Assorted buttons

_Assorted ribbons

_Beading needle

_Fray preventative

_Gold metallic gel pen

_Head pins

_Heart paperclips

_Large flower sticker

_Metal frame with vellum insert

_Old hat label

_Scraps of white vellum

_Thread

DETAILS:

● Use fray preventative on all cut ribbon ends. ● Trim the vellum with cream lace. ● Stitch the heart paperclips and beads onto the ribbon after the ribbon is adhered to the paper. Thread beads onto the head pins and then through the ribbon.

Little children are the most lovely flowers this side of Eden.

Rev. Dr. Davies

Lovely Flowers

MAIN PAPERS:

_BACKGROUND PAPERS:
    textured brown cardstock;
    musical score scrapbook paper;
    floral vellum

_LAYOUT PAPERS:
    brown, cream cardstocks

SUPPLIES:

_½"-wide brown sheer ribbon

_Adhesives

_Assorted gold buttons

_Assorted laces

_Brown rickrack

_Fray preventative

_Lettering:
    computer-generated
    or handwritten

_Scraps of white vellum

_Spray adhesive

_Tape

DETAILS:

● Adhere the vellum papers with spray adhesive. ● Secure the ribbons to the back side of the background papers with tape. ● Use the lace to frame the two photographs on the second page instead of the cream cardstock. ● Do not pull the knots in the ribbon tightly.

Marie

MAIN PAPERS:

_BACKGROUND PAPERS:
   dark blue, embossed
   floral cardstocks

_LAYOUT PAPER:
   tan cardstock

SUPPLIES:

_Adhesives

_Border stickers

_Embossed floral photo
   corner stickers

_Metal-edged label
   (center removed)

_Old hat beading
   and netting

DETAILS:

This is a beautiful photograph of my mother-in-law and her daughter. I had an old hat that had been disfigured, but I loved the beading on it. ● Carefully remove the beading from the felt of an old hat and adhere it to the page.

Hold a True Friend

MAIN PAPERS:

_BACKGROUND PAPER:
  daisy scrapbook paper

_LAYOUT PAPERS:
  cream, dark sage green,
  lime yellow cardstocks;
  assorted cream script
  scrapbook papers

SUPPLIES:

_2" head pins

_Adhesives

_Antique gold jump rings

_Assorted beads

_Assorted laces and ribbons

_Assorted stickers

_Brads with words

_Charms

_Embossed photo corner stickers

_Gold eyelet

_Heart brads

_Heart paperclips

_Laser-cut frame

_Laser-cut words

_Lettering:
  computer-generated
  or handwritten

_Peach colored scrapbook nails

_Ribbon buckles

_Scraps of white vellum

_Tiny metal frame

_Tiny tea pins

DETAILS:

● Copy some of the photographs onto colored cardstock. Then rip the edges to create the look of old photographs.

Abigail Evelina

MAIN PAPERS:

_BACKGROUND PAPERS:
  brown cardstock;
  brown floral on cream
  scrapbook paper

_LAYOUT PAPERS:
  cream, sage green
  cardstocks

SUPPLIES:

_⅛"-wide green silk ribbon

_⅛" hole punch

_5"-wide cream lace

_Adhesives

_Assorted beads

_Embroidery needle

_Gold metallic gel pen

_Label sticker

_Silver eyelets

_Spray adhesive

_Tape

DETAILS:

● Use spray adhesive to adhere the lace to the paper. ● On the back, secure the ends of the ribbon down with the tape instead of making knots.

Kiery's grandma has a small farm in her backyard. Kiery's dad takes them there to bottle feed the calves. They love to hold the great big bottle with the warm milk inside.

She has a large grassy field for the other farm animals to eat from. It is a wonderful place to run and play.

2000

S & K

S & K

MAIN PAPERS:

_BACKGROUND PAPERS:
pink plaid,
pink striped, tan,
tan floral cardstocks

_LAYOUT PAPER:
light sage green
scrapbook paper

SUPPLIES:

_⅝"-wide green grosgrain
ribbon

_Adhesives

_Alphabet stickers

_Assorted beads

_Border stickers

_Fray preventative

_Heart brads

_Heart paperclip

_Laser-cut flowers

_Lettering:
computer-generated
or handwritten

_Linen jute

_Metal butterfly sticker

_Needle and thread

_Scraps of white vellum

_Silver eyelets

_Tiny metal frame

_Transparent tape

DETAILS:

● Layer paper into strips on the tan cardstock. ● When beading in a long piece, adhere the jute all along the way or the string of beads will sag—take small stitches to hold up the jute about every inch or two. ● Secure the knots down on the back of the paper with tape.

fun and play

Only Girl

MAIN PAPERS:

_BACKGROUND PAPERS:
  tan cardstocks;
  lavender floral scrapbook paper

_LAYOUT PAPERS:
  cream, tan cardstocks

SUPPLIES:

_¹⁄₁₆" hole punch

_⅛" hole punch

_5"-wide cream lace

_Adhesives

_Assorted beads

_Craft glue

_Lettering:
  computer-generated
  or handwritten

_Metal alphabet charms

_Needle and thread

_Scalloped-edged scissors

_Silver brads

_Spray adhesive

DETAILS:

After discovering these photographs, I thought I would do some pages of my brothers and myself. I would like to think my daughter Sophie looks like me, but then again, it might just be the messy blonde hair. ● Adhere the lace with spray adhesive. ● Create the lacey edge on the layout paper with the scalloped-edged scissors and hole punches. ● Hold the photographs down onto the lace with a little craft glue.

It's Simply Girly

This chapter is full of ways to create with floral papers, laces, beads, and, of course, the color pink.

Modern Miss

Modern Miss Meikel

MAIN PAPERS:

_BACKGROUND PAPER:
  pale pink cardstock

_LAYOUT PAPER:
  embossed white
  floral vellum

SUPPLIES:

_½"–¾" assorted cream
    buttons

_½"-wide pink lace

_Adhesives

_Linen jute

_Metal alphabet letter

_Old hat label

_Scraps of paper:
    tan cardstock;
    natural scrapbook
    papers;
    floral vellum

_Silver jump ring

_Silver metallic gel pen

DETAILS:

● Don't be afraid to rip the edges of a
photograph. It gives the page a wonderful
dimension. ● Use the jump ring to hang
the letter from the knot of the jute.

Abby's Snowflakes

MAIN PAPERS:

_BACKGROUND PAPERS:
  pale lavender,
  white cardstocks

_LAYOUT PAPER:
  white cardstock

SUPPLIES:

_20-gauge craft wire

_Adhesives

_Beading needle

_Clear beads

_Needle-nosed pliers

_Silver metallic gel pen

_Thread

_Wire cutters

_Wire snowflakes

DETAILS:

Abby is my beautiful niece who is cooperative even on this freezing cold morning. ● Place the photographs on the background paper. ● Stitch the beads and wire snowflakes onto the paper. ● The letters were made with craft wire. Add a couple of beads onto the curves of each letter before curling the wire. Stitch the letters to the paper in a couple of inconspicuous places.

Her Favorite Place

MAIN PAPERS:

_BACKGROUND PAPERS:
   tan cardstock;
   floral vellum

_LAYOUT PAPERS:
   blue, pink, white vellums

SUPPLIES:

_Adhesives

_Assorted beads

_Beading needle

_Lettering:
   computer-generated
   or handwritten

_Spray adhesive

_Thread

DETAILS:

It's a wonder how I got any dishes done!
● Attach all of the vellum sheets with
spray adhesive. ● Use the pink vellum
under the wording for a little color.

her favorite place....

...the kitchen sink

Maren's First Year

MAIN PAPERS:

_BACKGROUND PAPERS:
    white cardstock;
    pink floral vellum

_LAYOUT PAPERS:
    light sage green,
    white cardstocks

SUPPLIES:

_$\frac{1}{16}$" hole punch

_$\frac{3}{8}$"-wide silk ribbon

_Adhesives

_Alphabet stamps

_Assorted green ink pads

_Clear beads

_Needle and thread

_Tape

DETAILS:

My gorgeous niece! ● To make the ribbon flower, punch hole for center of flower. Secure the end of the $\frac{3}{8}$"-wide ribbon on the back side of the paper with tape then pull needle through hole. Going out approximately $\frac{1}{2}$", insert needle into paper. Pull gently so there is a slight gather. Come back up through center hole and repeat for a total of six petals. ● Thread needle and add a bead to the center.

Paisley Baby

MAIN PAPERS:

_BACKGROUND PAPERS:
  cream cardstock;
  paisley floral vellum

_LAYOUT PAPERS:
  pink, white vellums

SUPPLIES:

_Adhesives

_Beaded necklace

_Needle and thread

_Silver eyelets

_Silver metallic gel pen

_Spray adhesive

_Tape

DETAILS:

I found the necklace at a dollar store.
● Connect with two eyelets and secure
the ends to the back side of the paper
with tape. If the necklace will not lay flat,
make a couple of stitches to hold it to the
paper. ● Hold the vellum papers on with
spray adhesive.

"Our Very Special Gift"

Natasha Michelle Lonni

Born August 7, 1999

Our Very Special Gift

MAIN PAPERS:

_BACKGROUND PAPERS:
  textured lavender,
  lavender berry
  scrapbook paper

_LAYOUT PAPERS:
  cream, white
  cardstocks

SUPPLIES:

_1½"-wide mauve lace

_Adhesives

_Beaded necklace

_Craft glue

_Green scrapbook nails

_Lettering:
  computer-generated
  or handwritten

_Needle and thread

_Scraps of white vellum

_Silver eyelets

_Tape

_Wire cutters

DETAILS:

● Use scraps of vellum to overlay the lavendar berry paper in the corners.
● Adhere the lace trim to the photograph and to the background papers with craft glue. ● Hold the vellum on with the scrapbook nails. ● Remove the ends of the necklace with a wire cutter. Hold the necklace flat to the paper with a few stitches. Pull the ends of the necklace through the eyelets and secure to the back side of the paper with tape.

Natasia's Buttons

MAIN PAPERS:

_BACKGROUND PAPER:
    tan cardstock

_LAYOUT PAPERS:
    light pink, teal floral,
    white cardstocks

SUPPLIES:

_Adhesives

_Lettering:
    computer-generated
    or handwritten

_Linen jute

_Needle and thread

_Scraps of white vellum

_Tiny buttons

DETAILS:

● Hold the name on with a couple of sewn-on buttons and accent with pink cardstock by placing under the vellum.

tip

Instead of just stitching with the linen jute, add a few buttons randomly at the points.

At eight months old Natasia is a chubby baby with chunky arms and legs. She has beautiful dark brown eyes and looks just like her daddy.
2000

Baby's Quilt

MAIN PAPERS:

_BACKGROUND PAPER:
  cream cardstock

_LAYOUT PAPERS:
  pink cardstock;
  assorted pastel
  scrapbook papers

SUPPLIES:

_Adhesives

_Alphabet stamps

_Antiquing spray

_Buttons

_Craft glue

_Ink pads:
  sage green,
  pink, violet

_Linen jute

_Needle

_Number stamps

_Silver metallic gel pen

DETAILS:

● Create a quilt pattern with 2" squares of paper. ● Refer to General Instructions on page 8 for the antiquing spray. Carefully spray some of the edges of the squares if not already antiqued. Adhere them on the background paper. ● Stitch the jute randomly around the quilt squares. Do not use too many stitches or it will become distracting. ● Adhere the scattered buttons with craft glue. ● Stamp the name and a couple of the numbers for the year. ● Add remaining numbers and matted photographs to the layout.

8 months

tip

*Don't be afraid to layer and
mix and match mediums.*

Baby Natasha

MAIN PAPERS:

_BACKGROUND PAPERS:
    tan cardstock; pink floral,
    textured pink
    scrapbook papers

_LAYOUT PAPERS:
    tan cardstock;
    white natural fiber scrapbook paper;
    floral vellum

SUPPLIES:

_¼"-wide peach silk ribbon

_⅜"-wide word ribbons

_Adhesives

_Assorted buttons

_Craft glue

_Lettering:
    computer-generated
    or handwritten

_Scraps of white vellum

DETAILS:

Keep it simple! ● Adhere the buttons and word ribbons to the paper with craft glue.

Sprinkles of Stardust

MAIN PAPERS:

_BACKGROUND PAPERS:
   pink, teal polka-dot
   scrapbook papers

_LAYOUT PAPER:
   white scrapbook paper

SUPPLIES:

_Adhesives

_Peach scrapbook nails

_Scraps of white vellum

Babies are sprinkles of stardust, little angels sent from above
A message from the heavens to remind us of their innocence and love.
A baby brings tremendous joy, but brings a lot of tears
To be a parent is the greatest gift and the memories last for years.

DETAILS:

● Soften the background with vellum. This page actually has three layers of vellum. The first layer is over the background, then there is a layer behind the words. The photograph is also on this layer. Attach a piece over the center with scrapbook nails.

Alison

MAIN PAPERS:

_BACKGROUND PAPERS:
  embossed floral
  scrapbook paper;
  green, floral vellum

_LAYOUT PAPER:
  tan cardstock

SUPPLIES:

_¹⁄₁₆" hole punch

_⅛" hole punch

_1"-wide light gold
  grosgrain ribbon

_2½"-wide lace trim

_Adhesives

_Fray preventative

_Lettering:
  computer-generated
  or handwritten

_Tiny metal frame

_Wave scissors

DETAILS:

● Cut the tan cardstock ½" larger than the photograph on all sides. ● Trim the edges of the tan cardstock with the wave scissors. ● Using the punches, create the "lace" edge by alternating the size of punches.

Emma's Primroses

MAIN PAPERS:

_BACKGROUND PAPERS:
   light blue, speckled cream cardstocks

_LAYOUT PAPERS:
   lavender, pink cardstocks

SUPPLIES:

_Adhesives

_Alphabet stickers

_Craft glue

_Flower eyelets

_Metal-edged labels (with vellum centers)

_Scraps of vellum: pink, purple

_Yellow brads

DETAILS:

● Adhere the alphabet stickers to vellum that fills the metal-edged labels. ● Make the flowers with five vellum petals per flower. Pinch each petal at its base. To give some dimension, crinkle the top of each petal. Place a small amount of craft glue in the center of the vellum tag and glue each petal into the center. Allow the glue to dry before punching a hole in the center of the flower, for the brads to be placed. ● Then adhere the tags into place with craft glue.

I was so excited when
I realized I had a beautiful photo
of my grandmother holding my mother.
I later found a photo of me
as a child in my mother's arms.
What a wonderful discovery.

1933 - 1966

Mother and Me

MAIN PAPERS:

_BACKGROUND PAPER:
   patterned ivory
   scrapbook paper

_LAYOUT PAPERS:
   cream, green
   cardstocks;
   musical score
   scrapbook paper;
   leaf vellum

SUPPLIES:

_1¼"-wide cream lace

_Adhesives

_Antiquing spray

_Assorted lace and
   ribbons

_Beading needle

_Beads

_Button

_Gold brads

_Heart paperclips

_Lettering:
   computer-generated
   or handwritten

_Peach scrapbook nails

_Scraps of white vellum

_Spray adhesive

_Tape

_Thread

DETAILS:

● Refer to General Instructions on page 8 for the antiquing spray. Spray a piece of white vellum. Lay it between several books until dry. ● Attach to the background paper with brads. ● Adhere the leaf skeleton with spray adhesive.
● Sew the beads right to the paper.
● Secure the knots down on the back of the paper with tape.

The Last Month

MAIN PAPERS:

_BACKGROUND PAPERS:
  two shades of
  moss green cardstock

_LAYOUT PAPERS:
  brown cardstock;
  natural leaf scrapbook paper

SUPPLIES:

_½"-wide brown sheer ribbon

_Adhesives

_Black permanent marker

_Gold brad

_Leaf skeletons

_Lettering:
  computer-generated
  or handwritten

_Pressed leaves

_Scraps of white vellum

_Skeleton leaves

_Spray adhesive

_Swirl paperclips

DETAILS:

● Adhere the leaf skeletons with spray adhesive. ● Note to the baby is inside the folded paper and is closed and tied with the ribbon.

A Little of Everything

This chapter shows how to create pages with layers, photograph layouts, a variety of mediums such as leather and metal mesh, with doors and flips, and the list goes on.

Grant Marcus

MAIN PAPERS:

_BACKGROUND PAPER:
blue cardstock

_LAYOUT PAPER:
blue natural fiber
scrapbook paper

SUPPLIES:

_⅛" hole punch

_Adhesives

_Antiqued defined
word sticker

_Assorted metal label
frames

_Gauze

_Lettering:
computer-generated
or handwritten

_Rectangular paperclip

_Safety pin

_Scraps of white vellum

_Silver brads

_Spray adhesive

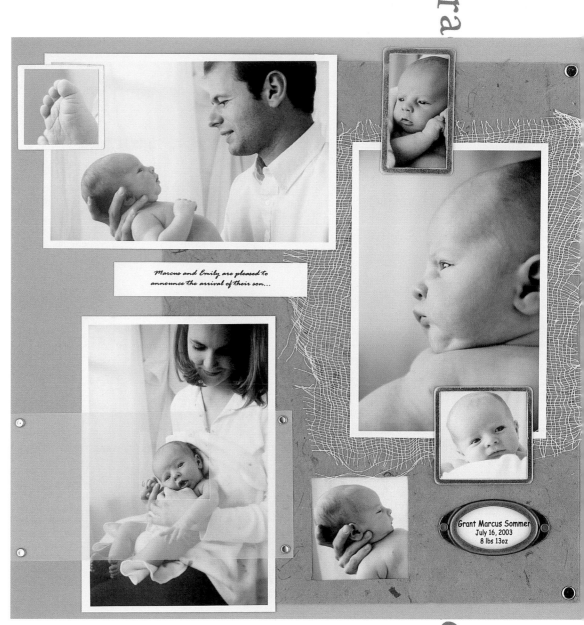

Marcus and Emily are pleased to
announce the arrival of their son...

Grant Marcus Sommer
July 16, 2003
8 lbs 13oz

DETAILS:

*My nephew with a dimple! He is as soft
as a pillow.* ● Create layers of frames with
the vellum, highlighting just the child's
face. Cut frames in the second layer to
reveal a tiny photograph underneath. ●
Cut out the lining in the frames. ● Use the
gauze as a nice texture for the baby. ●
Attach with spray adhesive.

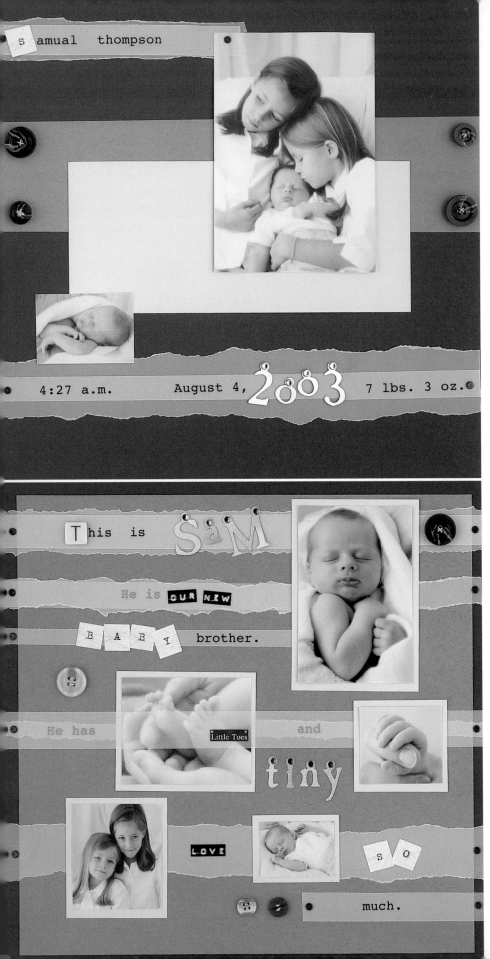

Brother Sam

MAIN PAPERS:

_BACKGROUND PAPERS:
    dark brown,
    speckled tan cardstocks

_LAYOUT PAPER:
    light blue cardstock

SUPPLIES:

_Adhesives

_Alphabet snaps

_Alphabet stickers

_Assorted buttons

_Bronze brads

_Craft glue

_Letter stone

_Lettering:
    computer-generated
    or handwritten

_Linen jute

_Metal alphabet and number charms

_Needle

_Scraps of white vellum

_Silver brads

_Word stickers

DETAILS:

These are proud big sisters! ● Create a story using the photographs and words. ● Weave the vellum over and under the photographs for a different look. ● After threading the buttons with jute, adhere on with craft glue.

Baby Sam

MAIN PAPERS:

_BACKGROUND PAPERS:
 green, plum, tan cardstocks

_LAYOUT PAPER:
 green cardstock

SUPPLIES:

_Adhesives

_Gold brads

_Gold eyelets

_Jute

_Metal baby foot sticker

_Metal letters

_Metal nameplate

_Safety pin charm

_Silver jump rings

_Wooden beads

DETAILS:

● Create the frame by cutting out the center of a smaller piece of tan cardstock.
● Adhere strips of the plum cardstock behind the framed opening. ● Add the eyelets and beads to the edge of the frame.
● Then adhere the frame to the background cardstock. Attach the nameplate and charm with the jump rings.

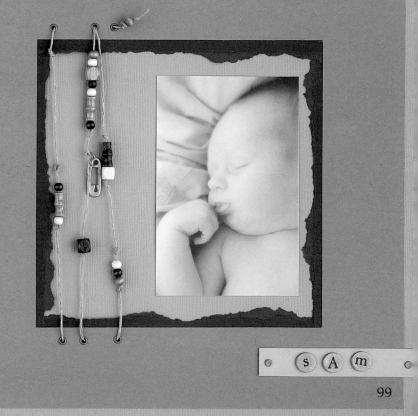

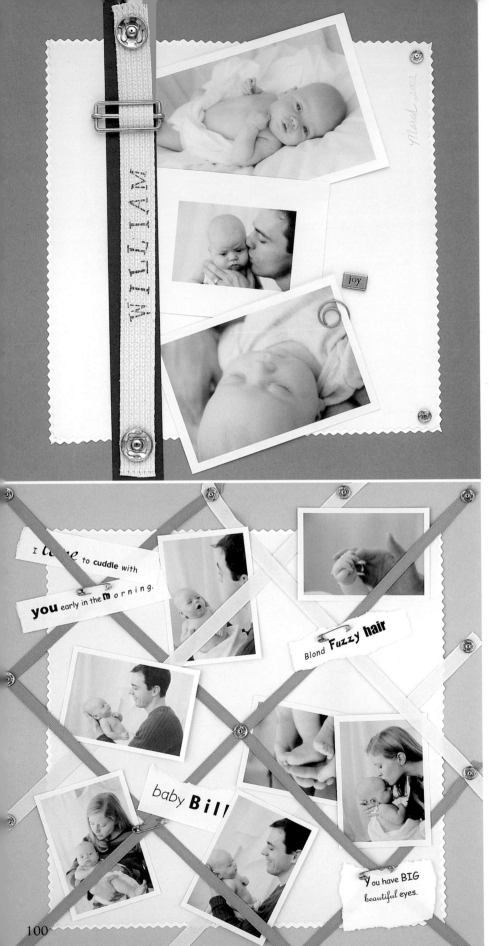

William's Note Board

MAIN PAPERS:

_BACKGROUND PAPERS:
   light olive green,
   olive green cardstocks

_LAYOUT PAPERS:
   dark green, pale yellow,
   white cardstocks

SUPPLIES:

_⅛" hole punch

_⅜" snaps

_1" snaps

_Adhesives

_Alphabet stamps

_Assorted grosgrain ribbons

_Awl

_Black ink pad

_Lettering:
   computer-generated
   or handwritten

_Safety pins

_Silver metallic gel roller

_Strap adjuster

_Swirl paperclip

_Word eyelet

_Woven trim

_Zigzag roller or scissors

DETAILS:

● Use a zigzag roller to create a decorative edge on the pale yellow and white cardstock. The roller makes a quicker, more even edge than scissors. ● Use an awl to punch through the ribbon and paper background before attaching the snaps. Write creative word sayings that describe your baby. Attach with safety pins.

Trace

MAIN PAPERS:

_BACKGROUND PAPER:
 patterned green
 scrapbook paper

_LAYOUT PAPERS:
 blue mesh, cream,
 corrugated cream cardstocks

SUPPLIES:

_Adhesives

_Alphabet stickers

_Assorted buttons

_Lettering:
 computer-generated
 or handwritten

_Metal label frame

_Metal mesh

_Safety pins

_Silver brads

_Tiny frame charms

DETAILS:

I've always wanted to use the index prints with the tiny photographs on them. What an opportunity to add them to this layout. The tiny frame charms were perfect for them. ● The mesh is a wonderfully soft texture for this baby. Attach with the brads.

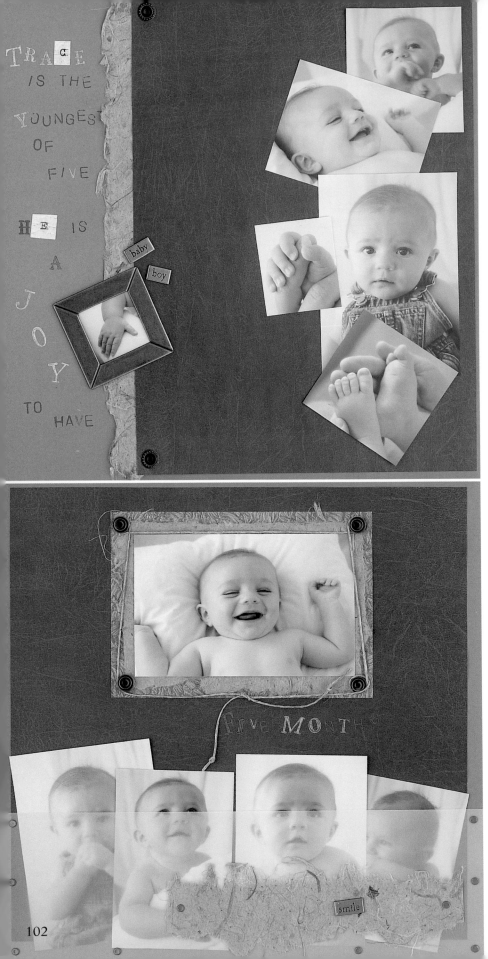

Trace's Smile

MAIN PAPERS:

_BACKGROUND PAPERS:
dark wheat cardstock;
textured brown scrapbook paper

_LAYOUT PAPERS:
brown natural fiber, cream script
scrapbook papers

SUPPLIES:

_Adhesives

_Alphabet snaps

_Alphabet stickers

_Assorted alphabet stamps

_Assorted metallic ink pads

_Gold brads

_Linen jute

_Scraps of white vellum

_Tiny metal frame

_Word brads

DETAILS:

● Adhere a scrap of brown natural fiber paper and word brad to the front of the vellum pocket, before securing it with gold brads. ● Wrap the jute around the alphabet snaps on bottom page.

Jacob Benjamin

MAIN PAPERS:

_BACKGROUND PAPER:
   dark brown cardstock

_LAYOUT PAPERS:
   medium brown,
   tan cardstocks

SUPPLIES:

_Adhesives

_Gold brads

_Gold metallic gel pen

_Lettering:
   computer-generated
   or handwritten

_Scraps of white vellum

_Spray adhesive

DETAILS:

● Type words and phrases in a variety of
fonts and sizes. Make extra copies to fill
in empty spaces. ● Layer the vellum to
add dimension. ● Use spray adhesive to
adhere the vellum.

My Little Man

MAIN PAPERS:

_BACKGROUND PAPER:
  textured brown cardstock

_LAYOUT PAPERS:
  textured green cardstock;
  natural fiber scrapbook paper

SUPPLIES:

_⅛" hole punch

_Adhesives

_Alphabet stamps

_Black ink pad

_Buckle frames

_Gold eyelets

_Jute

_Metal label frames

_Metal letter and numbers

_Silver brads

_Tiny metal frame

DETAILS:

● String the jute through the eyelets and tie on the front in a knot.

The Future Belongs to Me

MAIN PAPERS:

_BACKGROUND PAPER:
tan cardstock

_LAYOUT PAPER:
corrugated
tan cardstock

SUPPLIES:

_⅛" hole punch

_Adhesives

_Gold brads

_Gold eyelets

_Label sticker

_Leather alphabet stamps

_Jute

_Paper picture frame

_Scrap of leather

_Tape

The future
belongs to
ME!

DETAILS:

● Easily attach the sticker with brads. ●
Adhere the corrugated cardstock down first
before making all of the holes. ● Insert the
eyelets and lace the jute. ● Secure the ends
down with the tape instead of making
knots.

2½ yrs. old

Sam on Leather

MAIN PAPERS:

_BACKGROUND PAPER:
   dark brown cardstock

SUPPLIES:

_Adhesives

_Aluminum foil

_Gold brads

_Gold eyelets

_Jute

_Leather punch

_Metal-stamping alphabet
   stamps

_Scrap of leather

_Silver metallic gel pen

_Tape

_Wooden beads

DETAILS:

● The leather is perfect. Use a leather punch to create the holes. ● Refer to General Instructions on page 8 for embossing aluminum foil. Use the metal-stamping alphabet stamps on the foil. It is best to cut the foil after stamping to prevent running out of room or having difficulty centering the words. ● On the back, secure the ends of the jute down with the tape instead of making knots.

Ty and Lucky

MAIN PAPERS:

_BACKGROUND PAPER:
   gray-green cardstock

_LAYOUT PAPER:
   cream cardstock

SUPPLIES:

_Adhesives

_Black elastic cord

_Black nylon mesh

_Craft glue

_Number stickers

_Scrabble snaps

_Silver eyelets

DETAILS:

● This black nylon mesh is a great texture. Adhere it to the paper with craft glue.

tip

Use a combination of black-and-white photographs along with color ones. With these additions, the layout becomes a piece of artwork.

Trey

MAIN PAPERS:

_BACKGROUND PAPERS:
   dark brown cardstock;
   patterned orange
   scrapbook paper

_LAYOUT PAPERS:
   cream, corrugated orange
   cardstocks

SUPPLIES:

_Adhesives

_Gold brads

_Gold eyelets

_Jute

_Scrabble alphabet stickers

_Scraps of white vellum

_Tiny metal frame

DETAILS:

● To make the horizontal date plaque, fold over the sides of the vellum. Wrap ends over the jute, which is previously threaded through eyelets and attached to the background. Attach a brad through all the layers, enclosing the jute in the folded vellum.

Spunky Abby

MAIN PAPERS:

_BACKGROUND PAPERS:
   dark red, tan cardstocks

_LAYOUT PAPERS:
   brown cardstock;
   textured brown
   scrapbook paper

SUPPLIES:

_Adhesives

_Alphabet numbers
   and letters

_Brown shipping tag

_Hardware stickers

_Heart brad

_Jute string

_Metal-edged
   alphabet labels

_Metal label frame

_Safety pin

DETAILS:

*Abby is the youngest of six girls and has
the personality to keep up with all of
them.* ● Attach the safety pin to a sticker
and adhere the sticker to the page.

Reagan at Playtime

MAIN PAPERS:

_BACKGROUND PAPER:
 gray barnwood
 scrapbook paper

_LAYOUT PAPER:
 corrugated orange
 scrapbook paper

SUPPLIES:

_Adhesives

_Alphabet charms

_Lettering:
 computer-generated
 or handwritten

_Scraps of vellum

_Silver brads

DETAILS:

I wanted to use as many photographs as possible. Therefore, I cut several photographs apart to make 2" squares.
● Attach the letters with the brads.

OCT

2003

Reagan is our enthusiastic child with so much endless energy. He loves to run up and down the slide with little use of the stairs. His favorite thing to do is to "surf" down the slide, standing up, with anyone that will watch him accomplish this feat. He loves the camera and wants everything recorded especially on a digital so he can see his every move. He has a contagious smile that would warm anyone's heart.

...children at

Marcus, Sand & Trucks

MAIN PAPERS:

_BACKGROUND PAPER:
    tan cardstock

_LAYOUT PAPER:
    barn red cardstock

SUPPLIES:

_Adhesives

_Alphabet stickers

_Assorted of brads and eyelets

_Jute

DETAILS:

● Place the photographs before cutting strips of the barn red cardstock. Place the strips randomly around the background cardstock and under the photographs.
● Use the brads, eyelets, and jute for decoration.

playtime...

Be a Child

MAIN PAPERS:

_BACKGROUND PAPER:
dark red cardstock

_LAYOUT PAPER:
smoky blue cardstock

SUPPLIES:

_24-gauge silver craft wire

_Adhesives

_Aluminum foil

_Linen jute

_Metal mesh

_Needle

_Scraps of white vellum

_Silver alphabet stickers

_Silver brads

_Silver metallic gel pen

_Soft pad

_Stylus

_Tape

_Wire cutters

_Zinc swivels

DETAILS:

● Refer to General Instructions on page 8 for embossing aluminum foil. Attach the foil to the paper with adhesive or brads.
● Make holes in the paper with a large needle for the wire to be placed through.
● Use tape to cover the ends of the wire on the back side. ● A little adhesive may be needed to hold the alphabet stickers onto the mesh.

Rachel's Apples

MAIN PAPERS:

_BACKGROUND PAPERS:
  light blue, tiny floral,
  textured red cardstocks

_LAYOUT PAPERS:
  white cardstock;
  floral, red vellums

SUPPLIES:

_Adhesives

_Assorted buttons

_Craft glue

_Fray preventative

_Lettering:
  computer-generated
  or handwritten

_Linen jute

_Needle

_Scraps of white vellum

_Word ribbon

DETAILS:

Try journaling along the side of the page where there is extra space. I needed to do this because I ripped a tad too much off of the blue! ● First adhere the buttons into place with craft glue and then sew with the jute. ● Tie a bow on the top of the button from the leftover jute ends.

laughter

enjoy

happiness

delight

Hailey Marie

8 months old

laughter

Family Reunion Aug. 2003

114

Hailey Marie

MAIN PAPERS:

_BACKGROUND PAPERS:
    cornflower blue,
    speckled cream cardstocks

_LAYOUT PAPERS:
    cornflower blue, barn red,
    tan, white cardstocks

SUPPLIES:

_Adhesives

_Antiquing spray

_Blue brads

_Color copies of old nursery rhymes

_Lettering:
    computer-generated
    or handwritten

_Red eyelets

_Spray adhesive

_Word ribbon

DETAILS:

My mother has a 100-year-old book of nursery rhymes that was perfect for this project. ● Color copy them in different sizes and rip their edges. ● Refer to General Instructions on page 8 for antiquing spray. Apply the spray to the edges of the ripped paper. ● Use spray adhesive to adhere them to the background paper. ● Optional: antique the edges of the names to match the nursery rhymes.

Levi Tate

MAIN PAPERS:

_BACKGROUND PAPER:
   textured brown cardstock

_LAYOUT PAPERS:
   black, speckled cream
   cardstocks

SUPPLIES:

_24-gauge copper wire

_Adhesives

_Alphabet and number stickers

_Craft glue

_Denim belt loops

_Denim scraps

_Overall buckle

_Sewing machine

_Strap adjusters

_Wire cutters

DETAILS:

● Slide the strap adjusters onto the denim scraps before they were sewn onto the paper. ● Sew the overall buckle onto a denim scraps and then adhere with craft glue. ● Attach the denim belt loops with wire and glue. Refer to General Instructions on page 8 for attaching the craft wire.

Nathan's Envelope

MAIN PAPERS:

_BACKGROUND PAPER:
old envelope
patterned
scrapbook paper

_LAYOUT PAPERS:
green cardstock;
cream script, textured
tan scrapbook paper

SUPPLIES:

_Adhesives

_Antiquing spray

_Brown shipping tag

_Jute

_Number snap

_Silver brads

_Stickers: frames,
mailing labels,
numbers, stamps,
mini calendar

DETAILS:

● Create a door using folded paper as the hinge. The jute will hold the door closed. The door opens to reveal the photograph or journaling. ● Use the mini calendar sticker that represents the month in which the photographs were taken. ● Create the paper frame with an opening in a torn piece of paper. ● Refer to General Instructions on page 8 for antiquing spray. Spray the edges of the tag to give it a little bit more of a worn look.

Evyn in Autumn

MAIN PAPERS:

_BACKGROUND PAPERS:
    orange cardstock;
    autumn pattern scrapbook paper;
    leaf pattern vellum

_LAYOUT PAPERS:
    light brown, light sage,
    tan, white, yellow cardstocks

SUPPLIES:

_⅜"-wide cream grosgrain ribbon

_Adhesives

_Gold brads

_Ribbon buckles

_Scraps of white vellum

DETAILS:

When I found the autumn pattern scrapbook paper with the beautiful sayings and fonts, I decided I only needed one sheet. ● To complement the autumn pattern scrapbook paper, use the simple leaf pattern vellum to add the texture.

Evyn Marie
September 2003

thanks·giv·ing (thaŋks′giv′iŋ) *n.* [[ME <giving thanks>]] 1. a special gathering time for cherished family and friends 2. an opportunity for our hearts to reflect on all we are thankful for. *SYN*— tur·key (tur′...

[[ME *beauty*]]

au·tumn (ôt′əm) *n.* [[ME *beauty*]] 1.a brilli... palette of color 2. a crisp chill in the air 3... wonderful excuse to play in the leaves. *SYN.* scare·crows, har·vest, beau·ti·ful leaves

Three year old Evyn Marie enjoyed her day at the farm down in Salem. She loved the pumpkins and all of the autumn leaves under her toes.

Jonas at the Pond

MAIN PAPERS:

_BACKGROUND PAPERS:
    textured brown,
    tan scrapbook papers

_LAYOUT PAPERS:
    dark brown, textured cream,
    natural fiber scrapbook papers

SUPPLIES:

_Adhesives

_Gold brads

_Lettering:
    computer-generated
    or handwritten

_Scraps of white vellum

_Tan cord

_Tiny metal frame

July
2002

My name is
Jonas.
In july, my
mom and dad,
aunts, uncles
and cousins
went to this
castle place
to have our
pictures taken.
My favorite part
was when we
got to sit
on the dock
and splash
around in the
water.

DETAILS:

● Wrap scraps of natural fiber paper around the photograph and attach with the brads. ● Add additional pieces of vellum behind words on the vellum journaling, making a second layer and whitening the word areas.

tip

Use textured paper that will complement your photography and not distract from it.

David and the Ladybug

MAIN PAPERS:

_BACKGROUND PAPERS:
  navy blue, tan cardstocks

_LAYOUT PAPERS:
  light blue, navy blue,
  brown, moss green, burnt orange,
  rust, tan, white cardstocks

SUPPLIES:

_Adhesives

_Assorted brads and eyelets

_Black scrapbook nails

_Die-cut ladybugs

_Jute

_Lettering:
  computer-generated
  or handwritten

_Metal leaf plaque

_Tiny metal frame

DETAILS:

No one existed once David found the ladybug. ● Create ladybug wings by first cutting 1" circles out of the rust colored cardstock. Then cut the circles in half. Attach the wings to the ladybugs with scrapbook nails. Create an extra pair of wings on the flying ladybug by layering two half circles.

One *beautiful* autumn day...

David found a *lady* bug . . .

2003

...but then it *flew* away.

Spencer and Hunter

MAIN PAPERS:

_BACKGROUND PAPERS:
   textured tan cardstock;
   corrugated scrapbook paper

_LAYOUT PAPER:
   brown cardstock

SUPPLIES:

_Adhesives

_Alphabet snaps

_Antiquing spray

_Assorted buttons

_Embroidery needle

_Linen jute

DETAILS:

● Use antiquing spray on the corrugated paper's ripped edges if they are too white. Refer to General Instructions on page 8 for antiquing spray.

tip

Save the leftover scraps of paper. You may have an opportunity to use them for another project.

Little Cutie

MAIN PAPERS:

_BACKGROUND PAPERS:
    sage green,
    tan cardstocks

_LAYOUT PAPERS:
    light brown,
    sage green cardstocks;
    old box print,
    tan script scrapbook papers

SUPPLIES:

_Adhesives

_Alphabet and number stickers

_Assorted brads and eyelets

_Jute

_Lettering:
    computer-generated
    or handwritten

_Scrabble stickers

DETAILS:

● Add a little dimension with the appearance of doors. ● Create the "hinges" with folded cardstock and eyelets. ● Use the doors for extra photographs and journaling. ● Some of the doors may not open at all, but only give the effect of opening.

On the Farm with Gracin

MAIN PAPERS:

_BACKGROUND PAPER:
    barnwood brown
    cardstock

_LAYOUT PAPERS:
    white cardstock; cream,
    natural fiber scrapbook papers

SUPPLIES:

_Adhesives

_Alphabet tiles

_Alphabet stamps

_Bamboo paperclips

_Brown shipping tag

_Bug stickers

_Embossed paper daisies

_Ink pads: black, barn red

_Jute

_Metal label frames (centers removed)

_Mini calendar sticker

_Mini metal hinges

_Number stickers

_Paper border stickers

_Stamp stickers

_Tag stickers

_Tiny metal frames

DETAILS:

● Cut sections of the black-and-white photographs to be placed under the tiny metal frames. ● Use the mini calendar sticker that represents the month in which the photographs were taken.

Payton at the Barn

MAIN PAPERS:

_BACKGROUND PAPERS:
  speckled tan, tan cardstocks

_LAYOUT PAPER:
  natural fiber tan
  scrapbook paper

SUPPLIES:

_24-gauge craft wire

_Adhesives

_Alphabet snaps

_Alphabet stamps

_Aluminum foil

_Antiquing spray

_Assorted brads

_Black ink pad

_Brown shipping tags

_Brown trims

_Fabric binding ribbon

_Feathers

_Jute

_Lettering:
  computer-generated
  or handwritten

_Metal numbers

_Mini calendar sticker

_Paper picture frame

_Scrabble snaps

_Scrap of cork

_Scraps of white vellum

_Sewing machine

_Snap

_Stickers: alphabet defined words,
  key, labels, leather words,
  postcard, ruler, tags, words

(continued to next column)

_Stylus

_Washers

_Wire cutters

_Zinc swivels

DETAILS:

● Attach the elements in layers. ● Copy some of the defined words onto vellum. ● Stamp letters onto the fabric binding ribbon. It is best to machine stitch the fabric binding ribbon to the background paper. ● Attach zinc swivels with craft wire. ● Refer to General Instructions on page 8 for craft wire attaching, embossing aluminum foil, and antiquing spray the edges of the tags. Note: Refer to page 9 for the second page of this project, Payton at the Barn.

We waited to long to have Max come into our family. But what a wonderful wait to recieve such a beautiful child that has filled our lives with complete happiness and joy.

Max
Maxwell Duncan Sommer

MIRACLE

Beautiful Boy with Big Blue Eyes

MAX

LITTLE ANGEL

Blond Hair Crazy Blond Hair

100 0/0

PURE

CHUBBY

CHEEKS

We never could have dreamed this child could bring such a wonderful completeness into our family. Everyday is filled with laughter and enjoyment to watch him grow and learn new things.

Max's Crazy Blonde Hair

MAIN PAPERS:

_BACKGROUND PAPERS:
   textured tan cardstock;
   natural leaf, postcard
   scrapbook papers

_LAYOUT PAPERS:
   brown corrugated cardstock;
   brown-green scrapbook paper

SUPPLIES:

_⅛" hole punch

_Adhesives

_Brushed-silver brads

_Embroidery needle

_Lettering:
   computer-generated
   or handwritten

_Linen jute

_Metal number

_Scraps of white vellum

_Snaps

_Stickers: alphabet, number, word

_Word washers

DETAILS:

My nephew has the best hair!
● Randomly rip the natural leaf and postcard papers. Lightly adhere into place.
● Adhere the corrugated cardstock and ripped paper frame around the photographs. ● Stitch around the edges of the ripped papers. No need to be precise. ● Attach vellum lettering and journaling with brads.

Hardware Andrew

MAIN PAPERS:

_BACKGROUND PAPER:
  dark brown cardstock

_LAYOUT PAPERS:
  cream, corrugated tan cardstocks;
  natural fiber scrapbook paper

SUPPLIES:

_½"–2"cotter pins

_24-gauge craft wire

_Adhesives

_Alphabet stamps

_Aluminum foil

_Assorted brads and eyelets

_Assorted washers

_Key chain

_Metal mesh

_Metallic alphabet and number stickers

_Nuts and bolts

_Safety pin

_Scraps of white vellum

_Snaps

_Wire cutters

_Wooden screws

_Zinc swivels

DETAILS:

This was an adventure to the hardware store. What a find! ● Purchase the shortest screws so they don't poke out too far. Purchase the largest eyelets so the key chain can fit through it. ● Secure the metal mesh onto the background paper with the brads.

ANDREW

I am almost 3 years old. My mother took me over to Rebecca's house to do a photo shoot for a project she was working on. I did such a great job. We took a lot of pictures. She was very proud that I would say "No Thank You" instead of saying "no". She said that I was very polite.

SWEET BOY

AGE 2

OCTOBER 03

one year

Porter at One

MAIN PAPERS:

_BACKGROUND PAPERS:
  dark blue,
  tan cardstocks;
  textured tan
  scrapbook paper

_LAYOUT PAPERS:
  cream, tan
  scrapbook papers

SUPPLIES:

_⅛" hole punch

_Adhesives

_Antiquing spray

_Craft glue

_Lettering:
  computer-generated
  or handwritten

_Metal label frame

_Metal letters

_Scraps of white vellum

_Tape

_Tiny metal frames

DETAILS:

Can't resist the chubby hands and feet!
● Refer to General Instructions on page 8
for antiquing spray. Apply the spray to the
ripped edges of the papers. ● Tape the
vellum between the layers. ● Adhere the
metal alphabet letters (indicating the
child's initials) with craft glue behind the
metal label frame.

porter at one